AS LONG AS WE STILL LIVE

By:

Alicja Maria Zyrmont

The Military Biography of a Polish Soldier's Journey
Through Europe During WWII, 1939-1944

Podroz Polskiego Zolnierza Przez Europe Podczas II
Wojny Swiatowej: 1939-1944

'Kiedy My Zyjemy'

'Za Wasze Wolnosci I Nasza'

1 Polskiej Dywizji Pancernej

CONTENTS

DEDICATION

To my mother,

Margaret Barrie Lindsay Zyrmont - Pawlowski

who lived these pages

In respectful memory of EDWARD ZYRMONT, my father, whom I never knew, and who gave his life fighting for Poland, and in admiration of the courage and sacrifice of all the heroes of the 1st Polish Armoured Division, who died valiantly for our freedom and theirs.

ACKNOWLEDGEMENTS

The writing of this book required considerable research, and it is with much gratitude that I acknowledge those people who have been so very helpful to me, without their assistance this book could not have been written.

My enormous gratitude to the late Sir John Keegan for encouraging me to write this book.

The Polish Institute and Sikorski Museum, London, England, U.K.

The Ministry of Defence, London, England, U.K., who sent me my father's medals.

The Commonwealth War Graves Commission, London, England, U.K., www.cwgc.org, for telling me where my father was buried.

The 1st Polish Armoured Division, Veteran's Association, London, England, U.K., Commander Wladyslaw Lis, who sent much correspondence.

Kolo Kolezenskie 1-go Pulku Pancernego, Chairman S. Grabowski, London, England, U.K.

Polish Ex-combatants Association, London, England, U.K.

Borders Regional Council, Galashiels, Scotland, U.K., for records assistance.

McManus Museum and Art Gallery, Dundee, Scotland, U.K., themcmanusandleisureandculturedundee.com for displaying my father's military memorabilia.

Ministerstwo Kultury I Sztuki, Warsaw, Poland.

Bureau Central D'Archives Administratives Militaires, France.

Dr. Z. Wesolowski, Polish American Congress, Florida, USA.

Brian Olof, 'Easiguides,' U.K.

The Stanislaw Lazowski family, Gorzow, WLKP, Poland.

The Zbygniew Zyrmont family, Gorzow, WLKP, Poland.

My appreciation to my cousin Tomasz P. Zyrmont, London, England, U.K., tom.zyrmont@yahoo.com, for his invaluable assistance with Polish translations.

Thank you to journalist Michael Alexander from the Dundee Courier Newspaper, Dundee, Scotland, U.K., for writing a complimentary article about my work.

As always, I am indebted to author John Passarella at: info@authorpromo.com for his professional guidance as my webmaster throughout the past nine years.

Forever thanks to Todd & Julie Standage, Fountain Hills PC Repair, www.fhpcrepair.com, for helping me with computer tantrums.

A thank you to my lawyer, Rob McGee, Hudspeth Law Firm, rgm@azbuslaw.com , Phoenix, Arizona, for his legal expertise with copyright and contract issues.

Special gratitude must be acknowledged to the Telegraph Media Group Limited, who published a map of Poland in 1941, that my father carried in his breast pocket.

I am enormously thankful for the extraordinary help in formatting this book provided by Don Barar, don.barar@donbarar.com

A special thanks to my certified public accountant, James Maya, omycpa@aol.com for his friendship and support during all these years.

I would be remiss if I did not thank my husband of 42 years, Captain John J. Sullivan, a United States Air Force Vietnam veteran, for his assistance with military protocol.

And, I am very grateful to my beloved mother, Margaret Barrie Lindsay Zyrmont, for preserving my father's photographs for over 70 years, without them I would never have known him, and this book could not have emerged. At the age of 93 she read the manuscript and it was amazing to know that her long-term memory was still sharp; she remembered every incident experienced in this memoir, but she did comment that she felt there was 'too much of Margaret in the book.' I didn't think so because her strength of character and Scottish tenacity helped her survive the Holocaust and her Parkinson's illness. She died at the age of 95 on 24 February 2016, in Dundee, Scotland, before this book was published, but at least I felt she enjoyed reading the first draft while reliving some very happy moments of her youth, for she understood well and taught me about the bitter-sweetness called life.

My appreciation to my brother Michael, for using my poems in his English class - my first 'publication.'

Edward Zyrmont, for his priceless photography, which was the outline for his autobiography.

PREFACE

I have tried to make this military biography a human story, depicting the daily lives of the protagonists as they lived documented by original, never-before published photographs, from my father's Leica camera. My purpose was to present with clarity the personalities of these honorable men whom Hitler nicknamed the 'Black Devils.' Because they did not get the proper credit they deserved for their bravery and sacrifice in the annals of history, I decided to make them live again. ('To speak the name of the dead is to make them live again.' An ancient Egyptian belief.)

I wish my book to stand as a testament to these Polish heroes who fought and died to rid their country and Europe of tyranny; and it is with colossal gratitude that I thank all the soldiers who fight for our freedom today, and for their families' sacrifice.

This book was conceived solely from my father's photographs. When I turned them over and read the dates and places his story quickly emerged. However, to move the story along and fill in the unknown blanks, I saw the necessity of fictionalizing some dialogue based on my mother's recollection of true events. These yellowed photographs are a passport into the journey of the lives of people striving to live during a time when the world went insane. They document their hopes for a better future with patriotic dreams of freedom for Poland.

My father came from a poor but respectable family struggling to survive on a small farm in Wolkowysk, near Rozany close to Bialystok, on the border of Poland and Russia. They were grateful to God for their food and many blessings, but totally unaware that He would soon forget them. For their neighbors and priest on Sundays, it was a good life – until the Blitzkrieg and Russian betrayal.

I never knew my father, except through the legacy he left me of his collection of wartime photographs documenting his short life. My mother kept them in a leather bag for years never able to look at them again, so filled with poignant memories: 'N*essun maggior dolore che ricordarsi del tempo felice nella miseria.'* Dante. (There is no greater pain than remembering happy times while in misery.) There they remained dormant turning yellow over my lifetime yet shouting the truth of the suffering of millions of people, and how the war had torn my family in Poland apart.

Desperate to find out more about my family's past, I wrote a letter on 20 August 1976, to the British Red Cross in London, and they forwarded my letter to the Polski Czerwony Kryz in Warsaw, who had a letter from my family, now living in Gorzow, Wielkopolski. The British Red Cross informed me that my father had died on the 20t of August 1944, and was buried in the Polish Military Cemetery at Granville- Langannerie, France. The Polish Red Cross informed me that they had found letters from my grandmother and my uncle searching for me, but in

England. However, we emigrated to Argentina. Finally, after a lifetime of wondering, we had made contact.

For the 50th Anniversary of D-Day, June 1994, I travelled with my mother to France in search of the truth. All I had was Brain Olof's 'Easyguides' book, and followed his tour on page 70 of 'Operation Totalize.' I drove a Fiat with manual transmission getting lost in the French countryside while mother read the map upside down. But it was our fierce determination to visit my father that eventually led us to the cemetery on that warm summer's day.

I gasped at the sight of the sun shining on hundreds of grey granite crosses, and tears filled my eyes knowing I would meet my father for the first time, albeit at his grave. I was overcome with emotion. Mother found his grave first and placed red and white roses at the foot of his cross: Edward Zyrmont. Then she stood in silent reverence. She was only 24 when he died, and had never found out what had actually happened to him. Now here they were together again after all those years, and so much had happened in between. I gave them a few minutes together then walked over to his grave. How do I introduce myself to my dear father? How do I tell him that although both his legs had been shot off by a blast to his tank, I had won a silver cup in school in Buenos Aires for being the best runner? How do I tell him that mother had kept all his letters written in green ink in English, and that she had become an English teacher, and I had become a writer?

There was so much to tell him, but as I wondered about his story, the sun was slipping quickly behind the trees, and somehow I knew that there was no need for words. He must have been my guardian angel because how else did I survive despite the fact that Dr. Cora Campbell had told Granny Lindsay that I would not live through the night. Yet I had survived and lived to breathe fresh air, and had done well because he had sacrificed his freedom and died for ours; and writers, as free spirits, cherish freedom above all else.

Oh, how I wish I could talk to him, but destiny had cruelly robbed me of that right. His legacy to me apart from freedom, were his photographs which I dearly treasured, and because there were no negatives, I wanted to preserve his work, feeling the best way to do so and honor his memory was to write this book. He, and all his friends buried beside him, had fought valiantly for my freedom and theirs. They had died with dignity fighting to preserve their beloved Poland: their language, culture, history, patriotism - refusing the slavery the Nazis had forced upon them. It is for their valour I wish all of them to be remembered.

This is Edek's and Maggie's love story as they lived during the storm of World War II in Scotland, with authentic text, photographs from my father's camera, military records and documents. I wrote it so that the reader could have a comprehensive understanding of the epoch-making events through which ordinary people travelled. In it you will have an idea of what families endured together with the destiny of over three-quarters of the world's population suffering through the greatest fight in human history.

More than sixty million casualties, thirty million men, women and innocent children driven from their homes, and a massacre of thousands of Polish officers and intelligentsia at the Katyn Forrest, all because of a mad man named Adolf Hitler, and the support of the German nation, and of Soviet intervention.

The cost of war with its devastation and economic loss was estimated at over one billion dollars, not to mention the emotional scarring to people like Edward and Margaret, and the price Edward and his friends paid for human freedom. This is his story, and that of the 1st Polish Armoured Division, and the heroes of this regiment who fought bravely against the Nazis.

Having suffered personally from this holocaust, I feel a better understanding is necessary if we are to survive as peoples and nations whereby wars can be stopped at the point of their inception, so we can all live together in harmony and peace.

The obsession I felt by the strength of valour of the 1st Polish Armoured Division, and its heroic feats during the Battle of Normandy, in World War II, compelled me to document its heroism for future generations. And so, I also dedicate this book to those brave souls who paid the ultimate price, and their families who suffered without them. This is a true story of the bloody and dignified fight for freedom. I have endeavoured to make the book as authentic as the events unfolded, but my apologies to historians who might find something amiss, for it is the spirit of their humanity against all odds I am attempting to capture and remember.

PROLOGUE

'History is the biography of great men.'

Thomas Carlyle 1795 -1818

Poland is a very ancient nation that flourished in the middle of the 10th century, reaching its epitome around the 16th century when the Polish-Lithuanian Commonwealth was the biggest country in Europe. Its strengthening of the gentry and internal disorders weakened the nation, and in a series of agreements between 1772 and 1795, Russia, Prussia and Austria partitioned the country.

To comprehend the Polish character, which is the basis of my book, one must take several courses in complicated Polish history to understand that their survival as a nation depended entirely upon their patriotism and Catholicism. This is a proud country forged by continuous fighting to preserve its borders and strong national identity. Thanks to religious tolerance, it accepted thousands of Jews during the Holy Inquisition. It was the first country in Europe, and the second in the world after the United States, to pass a constitution on 03 May 1791.

Poland regained its independence in 1918, with the end of WWI. The newly reborn country was forced to fight to defend its border from a Communist-Soviet invasion of Warsaw, which it defeated in 1920. This is remembered as *'Cud nad Wisla,'* (Miracle at the Vistula.)

Just 19 years later, it was once again forced to defend itself from the invasion by Germany in 1939. Poles do not like to be reminded that the Nazis erected concentration camps on their German-occupied soil. Millions of Poles were killed, including my father, who is buried in a sea of crosses accompanied by Stars of David, at the Polish Military Cemetery in Grainville-Langannerie, France.

AS LONG AS WE STILL LIVE

Chapter One

1939 – 'For Your Freedom and Ours.'

On 31 August 1939, at 4:45 A.M., German units staged an incident, a false flag attack on a radio station near the border of the city of Gleiwitz, posing as Polish soldiers, without a declaration of war. Thirteen convicted criminals were taken from a concentration camp at Oranienburg in eastern Germany and placed in a schoolhouse to be held until needed for operation code name: 'Operation Canned Goods.' The German convicts were the 'goods.' This deception had two phases. On 31 August 1939, all but one of the prisoners were ordered to dress themselves in Polish uniforms supplied to them. Then they were administered fatal injections of a drug and transported to a forest near Hochlinde, about 10 miles west of the German-Polish border, where they were shot. Their bodies were placed in a scene to make it appear that they had died while advancing into Germany. Later, foreign journalists were brought in to view the evidence of this false attack.

The second phase of this farce was instituted later that same day. The remaining prisoner, escorted by Major Alfred Naujocks and five other members of the SS Security branch (the SD) were taken to Gleiwitz. This group, all wearing civilian clothes, burst into the radio station and commandeered it. One of Naujocks comrades speaking in Polish broadcasted an inflammatory statement announcing that Poland was attacking Germany, and calling all Poles to join in. Then, after a fight between the SD men and the

3

station personnel which erupted in confusion and shooting in front of an open microphone, the civilian-clad prisoner was killed and left lying on the floor to impersonate the 'Polish' broadcaster.

The following day, Adolf Hitler, in a speech before the Reichstag in Berlin, cited the charade at Gleiwitz as a cause of Polish aggression on German soil, and announced that he had ordered the might of Germany against the attacking nation.

After six years of bloodless triumphs over his enemies, both domestic and foreign, his assumption of power, the rearmament of Germany, the reoccupation of the Rhineland, the union forced upon Austria, and the seizure of Czechoslovakia, Hitler was ready to prove himself the Fuehrer of the battlefield. On 03 April, he had ordered his High Command to prepare an attack on Poland. The solution for Germany's many problems was to expand the living space for the people of the Reich, knowing it would be unattainable without invading other countries or attacking other people's possessions, and that this success would be impossible without shedding blood; and that first blood was to be shed in Poland.

The first shots were fired in Danzig in the Polish Corridor, which cut East Prussia off from the Reich. Polish control of the old Hanseatic Port had long been a source of resentment to the Germans, and Hitler felt it to be of symbolic value in its repossession of the first day of the war. On the morning of 01 September 1939, the Schleswig-

Holstein battleship fired on a Polish fortress, and thus Hitler staged World War II. The *Blitzkrieg* began with the first German bombs falling on the Polish Naval Air Force at Puck.

On 01 September 1939, the 35 million people of the 20 year old Republic Poland were aroused by German war planes dropping bombs on their homeland which would soon set off a catastrophic world war.

President Ignace Moscicki of the Republic of Poland, declared in Warsaw: 'Citizens, during the course of last night our age-old enemy commenced offensive operations against the Polish State. I affirm this before God and History! At this historic moment, I appeal to all citizens of the country in the profound conviction that the entire nation will rally around its Commander in Chief, and armed forces to defend its liberty, independence, and honour; and to give the aggressor a worthy answer, as has happened already more than once in the history of Polish-German relations. The entire nation, blessed by God in its struggle for a just and sacred cause, and united with its army, will march in serried ranks to the struggle and the final victory.'

This undeclared war was in direct violation of the Ten Year Non-Aggressive Pact between Poland and Germany Hitler struck five years before its expiration of 1944. Hitler's betrayal shocked the world; especially the United States of America, which harbored millions of Polish-Americans who adhered to democratic principles.

Then their reign of destruction struck on homes full of innocent women, children, schools, hospitals, churches, museums, libraries and fleeing people were machine-gunned down in the streets upon the orders of Adolf Hitler, a messianic world conqueror and the blessing of the German bureaucracy.

Adolf Hitler: 'Democracy is the disgusting death-rattle of a corrupt and worn-out system...the falsity of liberty and equality...I shall not be deceived by captains of industry...they are stupid fools who cannot see beyond the wares they peddle...damn your economic science...bring me money. I don't care how you get it....The world can only be ruled by fear....We are clinging to the old bourgeois notions of honor and reputation. It will be unbelievably bloody and grim. Yes, we are barbarians, we may fail, but if we do, we shall drag the world down with us...a world in flames. My purpose is the subjugation of all races and peoples and to set up our master race to rule the world...we shall be master of the earth.'

Nazism was not Hitler's invention. He stole it from Alfred Rosenberg, an anti-Christian, anti-Semite, and believer of German paganism. Hitler was born on 20 April, 1889, at Braunau, Austria, and suffered from delusions of grandeur, with a Napoleonic complex, who was driven to overcompensate for his inferiority complex. Vitriolic hate was his main personality. Hitler was nothing more than a common criminal, an uneducated charlatan and a common house painter, who with the support of the German people, rose to satisfy his own mad ambitions.

6

Germany was propelled by a greed of world domination, starting with Poland, in order to control a supply of raw materials essential for its armament. Hitler, a puppet of other forces behind him, also had his eye on Russia with its oil, iron, manganese, and other abundant materials, including agriculture and reservoir of manpower. But between Germany and Russia, stood proud Poland.

Poland had rejected Germany's insistence that it should join them in attacking Russia, and its reward would be a part of the Russian conquered territory. Poland refused! So, Hitler entered into a secret agreement with the Ribbentrop-Molotov Pact of 23 August 1939, seven days before the invasion of Poland. Another non-aggression pact the Machiavellian Fuehrer had no intentions of keeping. Just days after Hitler and von Ribbentrop tricked Russia into inactivity, Great Britain and Poland entered into a Mutual Assistance Agreement, signed by Lord Halifax and Count Edward Raczynski. Poland and France had been natural allies for many years. But it would take millions of men like Edward Zyrmont to finally extinguish the Holocaust Hitler's megalomania had started.

Chapter Two

General Stanislaw Maczek

Stanislaw Maczek was born on 31 March 1892, in Szczerzer, Eastern Poland. His military career began as an officer of the Austrian Army who fought on the Italian front in 1914. Following the outbreak of WWI, Polish units were organized around the cities of Krakow and Lwow, and this young officer offered his services to the new units of the Polish Army. His military talents were immediately recognized in the Battle of Lwow, under Ukrainian siege of 1918, and later in the struggle of the Polish Republic to stop the armies of Communist Russia, led by Marshal Budienny, for which he was highly decorated. Nazi Germany and the Soviet Union, under Stalin's orders, had signed a secret clause in an agreement: the Ribintrop-Molotov Pact, to eradicate Poland from the face of Europe. The Polish resistance was fierce as they were a stubbornly patriotic country, and would not be dominated or subjugated without a bloody fight by the nationalistic Polish army. But they were no match for the superior German military machine or air superiority.

Colonel Maczek's Brigade sped towards Spytkowice, where they came face to face with the German XXII Panzer Korps, under the command of General von Kleist. After a few weeks of valiant fighting on the 17th of September, the Soviet Union also attacked Poland's eastern frontier.

The 10th Brigade that Edward Zyrmont was in took part in vicious fighting at the Zboiska Heights, between 14 - 17 September 1939, against the German 4th Infantry Division. Maczek realizing the precarious position with the Russian invasion of the eastern border gave orders to stop fighting and depart Poland through the Hungarian border via Stanislaw, and to reach France any way possible to continue the fight with their old ally.

With the fall of France, Maczek was appointed by General Sikorski as first commander of the 1st Polish Armoured Division which was organizing in England. At the end of the north-west Europe campaign Maczek was promoted Lieutenant – General and Commander of 1st Polish Army Corps, headquartered in Forfar, Scotland. After the war, he was demobilized and lived in Edinburgh, working on the staff of the Polish Resettlement Corps.

He refused to return to Poland as long as it was ruled by the Communists. He and Field Marshal Montgomery did not get along since Monty had stated that he didn't mind if Russian troops remained in Poland, as long as they left Germany.

Maczek, despite being a hero, did not receive a pension from Britain or Poland, and was forced to work as barman at a hotel in Edinburgh. For his 80th birthday, Prince Bernhard of the Netherlands flew over for his celebration in gratitude of Maczek's, and the 1st Polish Armoured Division's liberation of Breda. On his 100th birthday, a group of his old soldiers gathered outside his home to salute him.

Lech Walesa promoted him to full general and awarded him the Order of the White Eagle, Poland's highest honour. He was also awarded the DSO in 1944, and appointed CB. His memoirs: Od Podwody do Czolga, (From Horse-drawn Wagons to Tanks), mentioned that Monty asked him: 'Do Poles among themselves, at home, speak German or Russian?'

He was married to Zofia Kurys, and they had two daughters and a son.

Chapter Three

1939 - Edward Zyrmont

Edward Zyrmont came from a happy family with three brothers, Mietek, Irek, Kazek, and a sister Helena. He was born on 14 September 1914 in Mogilowce near Wolkowysk (now Bialorus.) His mother's name was Antonina Pawluczek, and his father's name was Antoni.

He finished seven years of lower school in Rozana, and later attended teacher's college: Seminarium Nauczycielskie, in Slowina. When money was scarce he worked as a lock smith, and later joined the Polish Army on 02-11-1934, with the 2nd. Tank Battalion which took part in the campaign in Poland 01-09, to 18-09, 1939.

He had been a career soldier in the Polish Army for over five years, serving under the command of then Colonel Maczek, in the 10th Mechanized Cavalry Brigade. Maczek's Brigade of only 1500 soldiers and some weapons, crossed the Hungarian border in October 1939, under full colours. Not wishing to be interned in a camp there, he ordered his men to scatter and join him in Paris the best way possible so they could reunite to continue fighting the Germans under the command of General Wladyslaw Sikorski, Commander-in-Chief of the Polish Armed Forces in exile.

Zyrmont travelled to Hungary, and as pre-planned, the soldiers congregated in Orange, France. On 6 November 1939, when the Armoured Group was formed.

It was made up mostly of soldiers from former armoured units of Poland. At the Coetquidan Camp, it became the genesis of the 1st Polish Armoured Division, Maczek had dream of.

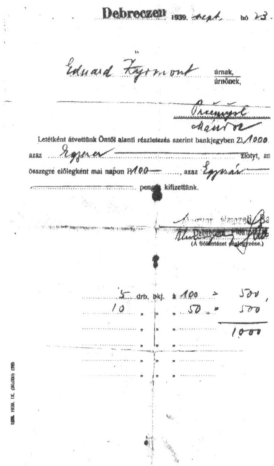

A receipt from the Magyar Nemzeti Bank in Hungary dated 23 September 1939, proves my father escaped through Hungary on his way to France to continue fighting with Colonel Maczek.

Colonel Maczek found his way to Paris and
reported to General Sikorski, who promoted him to the rank
of Brigadier General, putting him in charge of Polish units,
at the Army Camp in Brittany, France. During the winter
of 1939 and 1940, many soldiers escaped the poorly-
guarded Hungarian and Rumanian camps where they were
interned, and making treacherous journeys through Europe
succeeded in arriving in Paris where they grouped together
at Coetquidan Camp: *'Gzolgow I- Komp,'* under the
command of Major L. Furs-Zyrkiewicz.

Coetquidan Camp: 'Gzolgow I – Komp' - The genesis of the
1st Polish Armoured Division

Zyrmont came under French command on 20-10-
1939, and was posted to 1 Tank Battalion. The 10 Polish
Armoured Brigade took part in the campaign in France on
13-06, to 17-06, 1940.

After the capitulation of France 21-06-1940, he was evacuated by ship arriving in the United Kingdom on 24-06-1940, coming under British command on 01-07-1940.

France and Britain were signatory to an agreement which pledged military support in the event the Second Polish Republic was attacked. Once again, proud, independent Poland was to be sacrificed as in past history, but they would continue to fight for their independence now with an old ally, France, as there would be no question of surrender.

According to the military conventions between France and Poland, soldiers who were successful in arriving in France now were eligible to constitute a Polish Army in exile. Maczek immediately started creating his armoured brigade. The large surge of volunteers, some who came as far away as Argentina, and veterans like Edward Zyrmont, made it possible to quickly form an organization. Edek, a photo aficionado, was constantly taking photos of people. He was billeted with the Apolinarski family in France.

Avignon, France, January 1940
Edek's "war mother"

The Apolinarski Family, France 1939

Edek with his Leica camera and his best friend,Tadek Ruta

Edek and friends in France, 1939

France 1939

However, despite Maczek's best efforts, the French gave them ill-fitting uniforms and old Renault R35 and R39 tanks from WWI, giving them only 10 days to learn to operate them. Living conditions in the camp were bad due to the cold winter and the morale of the soldiers ousted from their homeland, and due to poor standards and lack of proper equipment.

The French government gave the Poles some old tanks like the
Renault FT-17 for their training so they could cover the French
withrawal near Diovon and Montbard.

Orange France,12 March 1940
Tank: Hotchkiss modified 39

Paris, France, 20 March 1940

Polish Soldiers in French uniforms

Polish soldiers in French uniforms billeted at Ste. Cecile les Vignes,
Orange, France April 1940

Tadek Ruta with Edek. Upset that he was given a WWI tank.

In February 1940, the Battalion left for St. Cecile les Vignes, where the 10th Motorized Cavalry Brigade was formed from all the armoured units.

Training in the mountains
Ste. Cecile les Vignes, 27 May 1940

On 03 March 1940, Edward (Edek) Zyrmont posed with his best friend Tadeusz (Tadek) Ruta, and a group of Black Moroccan soldiers in French uniforms in Orange, France, joining the 10th Armoured Brigade. Hitler derisively referred to them as 'Sikorski's tourists.' When not in training they spent their leave acting like tourists in Paris.

Polish and Moroccan soldiers in
French uniforms
Orange, France, 03 March 1940

'Sikorski's tourists' as Hitler
derisively called them.

French countryside, 1940

At that time, the Commander-in-Chief of the Polish
Armed Forces was General Wladyslaw Sikorski, operating
out of Paris, as Polish troops started arriving from Hungary
and Rumania. They were told that General Sikorski would
be their commander of the Polish Armed Forces in France.
'Gdy sloneczko wyzej to Sikorski blizen.' (When the sun is
higher, Sikorski is nearer.)

Still in training, Edek spent Easter, on the 25th of
March 1940, with Mrs. Apolinarski, his 'war mother' and
her family in Avignon. This kind and generous French-
Polish family harbored him during difficult times, including
inviting him to a Christmas dinner in 1939, just days after
his arrival in France. They also introduced him to Emilie

Kul Fren, a pretty French girl who obviously helped him learn French quickly. Photos given to him as souvenirs by Giselle, Yvonne, Mariette and Ellen, suggest he must have been speaking French fluently by then, as he certainly had a charm the French ladies liked.

Paris 1939

Paris 1939

These former armoured units moved to the village of Campeneac, becoming first an independent unit with the name of the 65 Tank Battalion, 1st Tank Battalion, and the 1st Armoured Regiment. Maczek organized his 1st Division on 02 December 1939. From there they hoped to communicate with the Polish resistance in Warsaw.

On their days of leave, the soldiers would walk around Paris. Edek enjoyed taking photos of different people, especially pretty French women.

Paris 1939

Paris 1940

Chapter Four

1940 - France Capitulates

When Germany attacked Belgium and Holland on 10 May, 1940, Edek's Brigade was sent to cover the French withdrawal. Major Stanislaw Glinski moved his battalion to Versailles. The Polish government in exile began negotiations with Great Britain, and with the catastrophe of Dunkirk, on 27 May 1940, thousands of Polish troops managed to escape to England to reorganize and continue their fight.

The 1st Company was ordered to airfield protection and the Finnish Company took its place. The 10th Motorized Cavalry Brigade, which Edward Zyrmont was a part of, under the command of General Maczek, deployed to Champagne on 08 June 1940.

With a blood-thirsty desire for revenge against the Nazis, this fledgling Brigade was placed on 06 June 1940, under the command of the 4th Army Group, with orders to cover the flank of the 8 Corps. These Polish soldiers were at the front but as a result of the German offensive on the 10th of June, it became a hopeless situation as the Germans had infiltrated behind French lines.

The 10th Armoured Cavalry Brigade on 12 June 1940, was launched at the Champagne front where it blasted the Germans around Champaubert – Montgivrous. On 13 June, still determined to fight, the Poles were bitterly disappointed when they were ordered to cover the French retreat in Romilly, suffering large losses. Lt. Col. Tadeusz Majewski, took command of the Battalion on 15 June 1940. With heavy losses inflicted on the enemy during the night, the enemy withdrew from Montbard. But this victory was short-lived for the Battalion was out of ammunition and fuel. The Battalion retreated to the south while under constant assault from the air.

An attack started on 16 June 1940, with the 4th Motorized Division in Montbard, Burgundy. Champagne and Burgundy were surrounded from the west. These units were being systematically destroyed from the air. The Battalion sustained heavy losses. The enemy aircraft broke the Battalion's first attack attempt. In the chaos which ensued, the Battalion retreated to the south while under constant assault from the air. Maczek ordered his tanks destroyed and told his soldiers to escape towards the south.

This temporary disbandment of Maczek's forces ended their part in the French campaign, but he was determined to reorganize his forces to continue his fight against the Germans. After only six weeks of fighting France capitulated. In June, General Maczek and Sergeant Kochanski, travelled by foot under the cover of darkness through the forests and vineyards of Burgundy, wearing their uniforms and armed, and reported to General Weygand for orders. But none were forthcoming.

On 14 June 1940, the Germans occupied Paris, and the French government asked for a ceasefire on 17 June, and French Marshal Philippe Petain signed the capitulation of France. The Poles were bitterly disappointed at their disastrous defeat as they were eager to fight on, but Maczek wanted them alive for another campaign.

To the Poles, the French capitulation was seen as indifference. The fall of France was terrible for them; their second but courageous encounter with the Germans only strengthened their fierce determination to continue the fight, as they refused to live under Nazi domination. For them, unlike the French, there was no question of surrender!

Petain was placed at the top of the puppet government in German-occupied Vichy, while Hitler visited Paris, and suggested that Poland should capitulate to Germany, as France had done.

Hitler severely underestimated the anger and determination of the 'Black Devils!'

Chapter Five

'Do Anglia' (To England)

On a grey and misty day in June, Zyrmont made his way south towards Vichy to the last ship: the S.S. Arandora Star, which arrived in St. Jean de Luz to rescue the Polish soldiers and take them to Liverpool, England. But since it was only a small fishing port and a large ship could not dock there, the only way the troops could get to the ship was with the help of the local fishing boats. The mayor of St. Jean de Luz had forbidden the fishermen to help with the embarkation because as far as he was concerned, France was no longer at war.

The Polish command was not too impressed with his rationale since they had lost soldiers defending France, and an argument soon ensued. This deadlock was broken upon the arrival of a Royal Navy destroyer. On it was a young naval officer who spoke fluent French to the mayor admonishing him that the destroyer's guns were directed at them. Unless, within ten minutes, his commanding officer saw soldiers being transported to the Arandora Star, his destroyer would open fire on the town.

'Ca va, ca va,' conceded the mayor, and gave his permission for the fishermen to start embarkation. They delivered 1700 men to the waiting ship and they sailed *'Do Anglia,' (To England,)* relieved and smiling for Edek's camera; very happy to be leaving France.

S.S. Arandora Star

Polish troops leaving France on the S.S. Arandora Star
20 June 1940

Edek leaving for England on S.S. Arandora Star.

The S.S. Arandora Star, was a British registered cruise ship operated by the Blue Star Line, from the late 1920s. At the onset of WWII she was assigned as a troop transport and moved refugees. One of the ship's officers wrote: *'The retreat down the French coast was becoming chaotic by this time and we were sent out to try and get down to the last port where there was hope of getting survivors out. This was St. Jean de Luz. All was fairly quiet when we got in, and we got about 1700 troops and refugees, including most of the Polish Staff and their troops who had been fighting back all the way down the coast. We got clear just as the bombers came over the hills, and strangely enough they left us alone this time! We went to Liverpool with that load, and lay off the landing stage while they were disembarked.'*

At the end of June 1940, she was assigned to transport German and Italian internees along with prisoners of war to Canada. On 02 July 1940, she was sunk in controversial circumstances by a German U-boat with over 800 lives lost.

Some of Edek's friends were not so lucky and ended up in German lines and taken prisoners. Others made it to North Africa where they were interned and forced to work on the construction of the Trans Sahara Railroad. Many had to overcome hard obstacles such as lack of money, documents, transportation, food, and took years to get to England. Some soldiers travelled via Russia to Japan, and to the U.S.A, or Canada, to regroup and continue the fight. But this was just the beginning of their struggle for existence.

General Maczek had also escaped as the Battle of Britain ensued, traveling through southern France, Algeria, Morocco, neutral Portugal onwards to Great Britain.

He told Sikorski he would build a formidable fighting force to win the war against the Nazis by rebuilding his brigade, but this time with another ally: Great Britain.

The soldiers were given names and addresses in England to report to people who would help them. The Poles arrived depressed and confused. Their orders were to regroup in eastern Scotland and prepare a coastal defence.

They were issued new British uniforms and rearmament was slow, but it was well organized as Britain stood alone against the Germans. Col. Stanislaw Sosabowski was given the command of the 4th Cadre Rifle Brigade, a formation that consisted mostly of officers without units, and was assigned the defence of the Firth of Forth, Scotland.

Chapter Six

1940 – Katyn Forest Massacre

During April and May 1940, Edward Zyrmont, had no news of his family or events occurring in his village so close to the Russian border. He kept a map he had cut out of The Daily Telegraph, showing Poland, and arrows pointing to a Russian invasion indicating how close they were to arriving at his village in Wolkowysk. He did not need a reminder of why he was fighting but he liked to show it to people to indicate his concern about the Communist encroachment, and worry for his family.

Unbeknownst to him and the rest of the world, in April 1943, Polish prisoners captured by the Russians were taken to Katyn Forest, 12 miles west of Smolensk, Russia. Iosif (Joseph) Vissarionovich Stalin, together with K. Voroshilov, V. Molotov, A. Mikoyan, M. Kalinin, and L. Kaganovich, signed a document favoring cold-blooded murder of Polish officers, soldiers, and other civilian prisoners.

Nazi Germany and the Soviet Union had invaded Poland and divided the country into separate spheres under the Molotov-Ribbentrop Pact. While the Germans massacred Jews and Poles in western occupied Poland, the Red Army arrested and imprisoned thousands of Polish military officers, policemen, and intelligentsia during their occupation of eastern Poland.

Those who were murdered in Katyn included an admiral, two generals, 24 colonels, 79 lieutenant-colonels, 258 majors, 654 captains, 17 naval captains, 3,420 NCOs, 7 chaplains, 3 landowners, 43 officials, 85 privates, 131 refugees, 20 university professors, 300 physicians, 200 pilots, several hundred lawyers, engineers, teachers, a prince and 100 writers. The actual number of the victims was 21,857, more than the usually mentioned figure of 15,000. They were considered 'hardened and uncompromising enemies of the Soviet authority.'

Stalin had systematically removed the best of Poland's intelligentsia: the intellectuals from the Polish military, political, artistic, social, and elite, whom he despised. About 700-900 of these victims were Polish Jews. This criminal act of historic proportions was part of Stalin's plan to prevent the resurgence of independent Poland. The Soviets lied and blamed this massacre on the Nazis, but the village eyewitnesses reported that the soldiers doing the shooting were wearing Russian not German uniforms.

Professor Stanislaw Swianiewicz was the sole survivor of the Katyn massacre. He was waiting to board a bus to take him to Katyn when an NKVD colonel pulled him out of line. Swianiewicz was an internationally recognized expert on forced labor in Soviet Russia and Nazi Germany, who had been born in Poland when it was still part of the Russian empire, and had studied in Moscow. He ended up in Siberia, and after the war emigrated to the U.S.A., where he taught economics at the University of Notre Dame.

In April 1943, in Katyn Forest, occupying German troops discovered large graves containing the remains of thousands of Polish Army Officers, still wearing their uniforms. Imagery from Luftwaffe aerial photo reconnaissance uncovered evidence of this crime and a Soviet cover-up. Among other things, it showed the area where the mass graves were located but had not been altered during the German occupation, and also displayed physical damage that predated the German's arrival. Eyewitness accounts from local villagers later stated that the soldiers doing the executions wore Russian, not German uniforms.

The Germans brought in an internationally-staffed medical commission together with some American prisoners-of-war, as observers. This commission determined that the massacre had occurred in 1940, when the area was under Soviet control, which information was then used as propaganda to disrupt the alliance between the USA, Great Britain and the Soviet Union. This effort was partially successful as Polish intelligence immediately blamed the Soviets for this atrocity which broke diplomatic relations between Poland and the USSR. The American response, at the time, was one of non-involvement. In June 1943, in a telegram to Churchill, President Roosevelt expressed his approval that the British approach to Stalin was grounded: 'Upon the obvious necessity of creating the most favorable conditions for bringing the full weight of the armed forces of all the United Nations to bear upon the common enemy - the winning of the war is the paramount objective for all of us; for this unity is necessary.'

General Sikorski demanded that the International Red Cross investigate this situation, but he was completely ignored, and later died mysteriously in a plane crash off Gibraltar.

It was not until 18 September 1951, when the United States House of Representatives established the Madden Committee to open an investigation to determine which nation was responsible for these atrocities. It found out that the NKVD was solely responsible for the crime. American officials had led a cover-up and ignored the Russian despicable behavior as early as 1943.

Years later, the absolute truth surfaced when the U.S. National Archives requested declassification of documents, and photographs about the Katyn Forest massacre, and then released them together with photos to the Polish nation and the rest of the world.

Chapter Seven

1940 – Great Britain

The fall of France was depressing for the Polish cause. Their brief, but valiant contact with the enemy only made their quixotic dream more resolute: 'A free Poland!'

General Maczek had escaped with some soldiers and Sgt. Kochanski, on foot by night through the forests of Burgundy. He left via Tunis, French Morocco, and Gibraltar, with his companions via Marseilles, Barcelona, Madrid and Lisbon, to meet up in Douglas, Scotland, to join the Polish 10th Armoured Cavalry Brigade, which was being reorganized for the second time during the war.

Edward Zyrmont had fought his way out of Poland and France, and his determination had not vanquished, but it was time for a badly needed rest. He was told to find the Polish General Consul in London. Somebody had written on the back of a photo: '63 Portland Place, London, W1.' On another photo of a very depressing winter scene somebody had scribbled: 'Miss Priese, 106 Frogmore Road.' He used his photos as if they were business cards, and had the habit of writing on the back of them.

Konsulat Generalny
Rzeczpospolity Polskie
63, Portland Place
London W.1.

MISS PRUESE
106 FROGMORE RD

On the back of this photograph,
someone had written: '63 Portland
Place, London W.I', as their contact
for assistance.

In Liverpool the soldiers were met by the Women's
Voluntary Service, offering them tea and sandwiches, then
sending them on to trains to Scotland. In his typical
charming fashion, Edek began conversations with the
friendly women in his sparse English vocabulary and the
aid of a Polish-English dictionary, and relied upon a lot of
gestures to communicate.

The Women's Voluntary Service met the soldiers as they arrived in England, gave them tea, sandwiches, and took them to the railway station.

Women Voluntary Service England 1940	Edek and Tadek Lanarkshire, England, 1940

By July 1940, nearly 16,000 Polish troops arrived in Great Britain. The War Office decided to send them to Scotland where they could begin reorganizing as Maczek had wanted. The English people were very friendly to the Poles, but the Scots were exceptionally hospitable and warm, and they soon developed a strong affinity. Their defeat by the Nazis in Poland and France did not seem to dampen their effervescent spirits. They were hopeful and optimistic that Britain would be their salvation, and that of their beloved homeland. They quickly developed a rapport with this friendly nation, which assisted them in organizations such as the City Corporation opening canteens, and permitting them to travel for free on their tramcars.

ODZNAKA PAMIATKOWA
I PUŁKU PANCERNEGO

LEGITYMACJA

Nr. 195

Chapter Eight

1940 - Scotland

Touring Glasgow, Edek and his best friend Tadek, were not shy about taking pictures with Greta who gave him a picture of herself wearing a kilt, and with typical Scottish warmth signed it, 'To Edek, love from Greta.' By now he was wearing one of his medals and inviting another Scottish lass to ride on his motorbike, for Edek had a way with women!

To Edward from Greta with love, Glasgow.
Scotland, 1940.

Glasgow, 1940

During the first few weeks of their arrival in the land of the thistle, the Poles made quite a quixotic impression upon the local gentry. Their titled senior officers tended to kiss the hands of the women, click their heels, smell of French cologne, use cigarette holders, and with foreign elegance won over the local ladies who did not hesitate to invite them into their homes for tea and sympathy. Mrs. Margaret Taggart, was particularly hospitable, and invited Edek and Tadek to tea.

Tea with Mrs. Taggert. Glasgow, Scotland
21 December 1940

Now in a British Army uniform, as Edek lay in his
cot at night in his damp tent, he often wondered and
worried about the fate of his mother Antonina, sister
Helena and three brothers: Irek, Mietek and Kazik, left
behind on their tiny farm. What had become of them? How
were the Russians treating them? He was quite concerned
as he did not trust the Russians any more than he trusted the
Germans. This war for him was very personal, and he was
eager to get back at the Nazis for destroying their lives.
With an obstinate Polish mind he dreamed of revenge.
Damn Montgomery! They were ready to fight now, not
when the war was over! But Montgomery insisted the

Polish Armoured Division was still too green to be taken seriously. This was of enormous frustration to the Poles as they were anxious for their revenge. They wanted blood!

Edek in a British uniform Scotland, 1940	The War Office sent the Poles to Crawford to begin training. Crawford, Scotland, 1940

Studying English on maneuvers.

Edek and Tadek now in Scotland

Edek's English was improving as he diligently studied his grammar books at night. His French was quite good as he had studied it in school, but English was a challenge for him. He had met some interesting French women, and now was meeting some very pretty Scottish lassies who had invited him to their homes for tea and shortbread; but this weekend he was in need of some – whisky.

Edek's friends in Scottland.

Jean Ashe, Maggie and Bette Lindsay

Chapter Nine

1940 – Dundee, Scotland

Soon equipment and British uniforms started arriving and tents were provided for the soldiers. Despite the initial tough living conditions of sleeping in tents, later their accommodations improved somewhat as they were issued Nissen huts to sleep in. The 'laughing barrels' as the Poles called them because of their wine barrel shape, but at least they kept them out of the rain and the cold Scottish fog.

'The Laughing Barrels' (Nissen Huts) where Polish soldiers were billeted.

Even living in tents and huts did not deter Edek's pride. He was vain about his appearance and commissioned a Polish tailor to sew a seam down the middle of his trousers so that they always looked neatly pressed. As the months flew by, regardless of difficulties, language barrier and uncomfortable living conditions, soon two infantry brigades were born. The 1st was based in

Biggar, and the 2nd in Douglas, and a small armoured group soon emerged.

The Palais Dance Hall, Dundee

The Palais Dance Hall in Dundee, with its big band, plenty of whisky and friendly women was just the distraction Edek needed from this bloody war. He walked over to the bar with his best friend Tadek Ruta, and lit a Senior Service cigarette, and ordered a whisky as the orchestra played an Artie Shaw melody. It was a busy Saturday night and the place was packed with all kinds of uniforms. Outside, as usual, it was raining. While the band took a break, a tall brunette walked over to the piano with another perky girl and started playing a medley of songs. The younger one started singing quietly as the prettier one with the long, slim fingers played, 'Ma, He's Making Eyes at Me.'

As a couple of men in RAF uniforms approached the piano, Edek winked at Tadek, 'Let's go over and show those fly boys our singing talents.'

'But I can't sing in English,' Tadek protested laughing.

'Then we will sing in Polish!' Edek said ordering another whisky placing it on the piano for the attractive brunette. 'Good evening, would you like this whisky?'

She ignored him. His smile was too inviting. Within minutes Army uniforms with 'Poland' on their sleeves and a feathered-helmet badge in an orange circle on their left shoulders, and some RAF uniforms all circled the piano.

'Let's buy the pilots from the 303 Squadron a drink. They deserve our cheers for being the highest scoring Allied unit. They are bashing Goering's Heinkels. Our Spitfires are going to eat them for lunch!' Edek told Tadek, happy the RAF had shot the hell out of the Luftwaffe.

'Do you know any Polish songs? Edek asked the pretty piano player.

'No. But if you start singing, I will pick up the tune.' She smiled up at him, accepting his drink.

'My sister plays by ear. She can play anything you sing or hum. She follows along, but her left hand for the chords is not so great.' The younger girl chirped in.

Suddenly a chorus of male voices broke into Polish songs as Maggie tried to keep up with the melodies she heard for the first time. By the second chorus, she had the music in her mind. The Army was trying to sing louder than the RAF, and Edek out-sang them all with his pleasant baritone voice. Tadek shouted along off-key while the pianist struggled to keep up. Her left hand not quite mastering the chords of the unknown melodies.

Seeing the band members pick up their instruments, she motioned that the impromptu sing-along had come to an end. Edek asked the pretty pianist if she would like to dance with him. 'I am pleased to meet you. I am Edward Zyrmont,' he said kissing the back of her hand clicking his heels.

'And I am Margaret Lindsay,' she answered noticing he was strikingly handsome with his thick shock of brown hair framing a devilish smile. As they moved slowly to 'Dancing in the Dark,' she felt his velvety brown eyes settle deeply on hers.

'My friends call me Edek,' he said. 'Would you like to join me with your friend, and my friend Tadek at our table for a drink?' He asked politely hoping she would not decline.

While the orchestra started playing '*I'll Never Smile Again,*' the conductor announced: 'Ladies and gentlemen, I will now sing for you a Tommy Dorsey hit, and I will try my best Frank Sinatra tonsils. Since Frankie can't be with us tonight, I'll fill in for him.' He laughed acknowledging the applause.

'I am with my sister Bella, who is somewhere around here,' Maggie replied noticing his trousers had a straight line down the middle, his hair was impeccable groomed, and he had the manners of a titled gentleman.

'May I call you Lin for short?' He teased. 'You have such beautiful blue eyes.' He said whisking her off to dance to the tune of '*All the Things You Are.*'

Without missing a beat, the orchestra started playing *'Dancing in the Dark.'* 'My sisters call me Maggie. Sometimes Meg if they are angry with me. You are a fantastic dancer, Edek. Where did you learn to dance so well?' She noticed he had a very broad smile.

'I spent some time in Paris. I enjoy dancing while holding a lovely girl in my arms. The Argentine tango is all the rage now. Did you see the film *'Tango Bar'* with Carlos Gardel?'

'No. Was it any good?' She glanced around the room looking for Bella. She hoped she had picked up their two gas masks off the piano, and placed them on the chairs. They would need them to walk home as soon as curfew was announced.

'The music was fantastic, but I preferred *'Adios Buenos Aires,'* it was full of tangos and I concentrated on the steps. That's how I learned how to do it with the twists and dip,' he said stretching his arm in the air like a matador. When the music stopped they walked back to their table. But Bella was nowhere to be found.

'If they show those films again, I would like to see them.' Maggie said with a cigarette in her mouth reaching into her handbag for a match, but he immediately took out his lighter and lit it for her.

'Will you take me to Buenos Aires?' She blew smoke away, leaning in towards him laughing. 'Do you speak Spanish too?'

'No. Only Polish and French. I apologize for my broken English, I am still learning it. Will you teach it to me?' He smiled. 'I bought some records in France. Do you have a gramophone at home?'

'Yes. We always have music on at home. If the wireless is not on, my sister Jess – she is the eldest – plays the piano beautifully. She took lessons. She can even play Chopin. But there was no money left over for me to take instructions.' She waved to Bella on the dance floor to come and join them.' he said confidently, excusing himself, walking over to the conductor.

'Ladies and gentlemen, by special request, we will play an Argentine tango.' The conductor announced picking up his baton as Edek rushed across the room to get his 'Lin' onto the dance floor. As the sensuous strains of the tango filled the hall, he clasped her tightly by the waist to guide her in the intricate steps.

'Just follow me. It is not so difficult. Walk rhythmically to the music - like this.'

'Ow! Your medal is scratching me.'

He pushed away. 'Sorry!'

'What did you get that for? Did you kill many Jerries?'

'For the campaign in France. No. I didn't get as many Germans as I would have liked.'

'Well, the war isn't over. You will still have your chance.'

Edek's face changed expression. He was dancing with a woman who looked like Hedy Lamarr, and he did not want to talk about war at this particular moment. Not since Paris had he held the softness of a woman in his arms. He inhaled deeply the clean, sweet lavender perfume in her long, dark hair framing her lovely blue eyes.

As the tango music continued, he carefully studied her features. Her eyes were a cornflower blue starred with thick black lashes. Above them, her eyebrows rounded emphasizing her pretty face.

Only a few other dancers dared to join in, for most were still learning the complex steps and were watching Edek and Maggie twist and gyrate around the floor under the colored lights, as if the world belonged only to them.

Maggie laughed out loud, throwing her head back, 'It isn't that difficult once you get the hang of it, just don't dip me to the floor!'

When the music stopped, they both sat down out of breath as Edek ordered more drinks. 'Have you seen your sister yet?' He asked her handing her a gin and tonic as he stayed with whisky, while the band started playing '*Boogie Woogie Bugle Boy.*'

'There she is! She is the short one bouncing about with that RAF uniform.' She pointed with her cigarette. 'She is one of our singers in the family.'

'She looks to me like she is also quite a dancer.' He waved to Tadek across the room, but he was too busy talking to a redhead to acknowledge him. 'Do you sing also?'

'Heavens no! I have a terrible voice. So I was told at school. But my older sister, Elsie, has a lovely voice. Sometimes she sings opera and keeps quite busy with concerts, and sings at weddings. Jean also has a very nice singing voice.'

'How many sisters do you have?'

'Five. There is Jess, Elsie, Jean, Bella, Bette. I also have three brothers, James, George, and Bobby, who is the youngest. With me we are nine altogether.'

'I too come from a big family, but not as big as yours. I have a sister Helena and three brothers, Irek, Mietek and Kazik.' He said pensively crushing his cigarette butt in the ashtray with a far-away look on his face wondering how they were all doing.

'They are playing a waltz. Do you mind if we dance, Edek?' She said getting up from the chair.

While they twirled and twirled around avoiding bumping into other dancers who had flooded the floor, they smiled at each other looking into each other's eyes without a care in the world forgetting about the ravages of the war outside. Tonight there was only music, drink, laughter and friendships.

'One last dance before closing time,' the conductor announced playing *'You Made Me Love You'*, as the lights flickered, reminding everyone it was near curfew time and leave the escape of the romantic dance hall to enter the brutal reality of bombs and death.

Edek held her closer, 'I am going to marry you!' he whispered in her ear.

'Don't be silly. You know nothing about me.' She smiled obviously enjoying his outrageous advances, but not daring to laugh as there was something in the tone of his voice that told her he was very serious.

'I know you have sky blue eyes, are tall, nice legs, are a good dancer, a fantastic piano player, and that you come from a big family. What else do I need to know?' He smiled convincingly not the least dissuaded by her indifference.

'Are you Poles always this gallant?' She said slipping into the folds of her woolen coat, flattered by his absurd proposal which she did not take seriously, despite her twenty years of age.

'Always.' He said helping her on with her coat.

'Maggie, I have been looking for you everywhere.' Her sister said out of breath.

'Meet Edek Zyrmont, my future husband,' she laughed. 'This is my sister, Isobel, but we call her Busy Bella.'

'Charmed, I'm sure.' She curtsied mockingly giving him the once over smirking, going along with the joke. 'Am I invited to the wedding?' She giggled slipping her arm into her coat while Edek helped her put it on.

'I am very happy to meet you, Bella,' he said kissing the back of her hand, clicking his heels.

'Here are the gas masks. You left them on top of the piano but I rescued them.' Bella handed her one.

'Will you be here next Saturday?' Edek eagerly wanted to know when the music stopped. The lights came back on full strength as uniforms and young women rushed out the front door before curfew promising to see each other again.

'Yes. We like to come to improve our dancing. Now I can dance the tango,' Maggie responded proudly.

'Before you go, would you like to give me your address? I don't want to lose contact with you – in case you are not here next week. How can I marry you if I can't find you?' He winked, pulling out a photo from his pocket writing her address on the back of it.

As the two Lindsay sisters linked arms huddling closer, quickening their pace to keep out the cold damp air, they hastened towards home. 'Where did you find your

Lawrence Olivier? He looks just like him.' Bella asked through chattering teeth, shivering in the foggy night.

'He found me while I was playing the piano. Who was that good looking Pole you were dancing the night away with?' Maggie asked, pulling up her collar around her frozen ears.

'His name is Stefan. My feet are killing me with these shoes.' No sooner had she finished her sentence when a motorbike came to a screeching halt in front of them scaring the life out of them.

'Lin!' Edek yelled over the noise of his engine, 'I want to see you next Friday night, if you are not busy. How would you like to see *'Lady of the Tropics'*, with Hedy Lamarr?'

'Tropics? Sounds nice and warm. Where I'd like to be right now!' Maggie answered pulling the collar of her coat around her ears, thinking of traveling to South America some day when the war was over. Anxious to get out of the chilling night air and home to her warm bed, she quickly agreed. 'All right - we can meet at the park next to the Queen's Hotel.'

'How about at nineteen hundred?' He asked with urgency in his voice.

'Seven o'clock is fine. I get off work at noon. Bye Edek.' She replied fantasizing of traveling someday to South America and to a much warmer climate.

'Perfect! We can have a drink at the hotel before the film. Then go next door to the cinema.' He tilted his black beret and sped off like a knife slicing through the thick mist for the blackout was on and the war had not gone away. It had only disappeared for a few magical moments, but was ever present.

Bella looked up at her taller sister, 'Why did he call you Lin?' She asked in amusement thinking her sister was playing one of her make believe games since she had always wanted to be an actress. 'You should have told him your name was Marguerite, as in '*La Dame Aux Camelias.*'' Bella made a histrionic gesture with her gloved hand.

'He just came up with that name, short for Lindsay. These Poles are a funny bunch! They are so full of fun!'

'Then we can be too.' Bella giggled, sticking her hands down further into her pockets searching for more warmth as the fog was getting thicker while they hastened their steps trying to keep warm, almost home.

The sisters were glad to see their mother waiting up for them. 'Did ye hae a bra time?' She wanted to know putting on the kettle. She thought a 'cuppa tea' was the panacea that cured every ill imaginable from broken bones to broken hearts. Even the war stopped for the British Isles at exactly four o'clock every afternoon while they enjoyed their tea. For the British were traditionalists at heart and were not about to change their lifestyle just because Hitler wanted their country.

'Yes, ma. We met a couple of dashing Polish soldiers, and Edek wants to marry her. He calls her Lin. Isn't that ridiculous!' Bella said enthusiastically. 'My lad is Stefan and he is more serious than Edek, but he is awfy charming.'

'I'm meeting Edek next weekend,' Maggie interjected, 'he was really taken with me.' She said warming her hands at the dying embers of the fire. 'I see the fire has gone out. I'll nae be lang to my bed. Did you put the hot water bottle in it? Dancing the tango made me move muscles I didna ken I had!'

'Edek - Stefan – tango, can't you find a couple of Scottish lads yer ain kind, with names I can prronounce and dance the highland fling? I'll nae underrstand a worrd they say - these forreigners.' She shook her head. 'Yes, I put the hot waterr bottle in yerr bed and a couple of auld coats on top of it tae keep ye warrm. I'll be glad when this warr is overr.' She said in a thick Scottish brogue, thinking about her two boys in uniform. George was training in Canada, and Jimmy was somewhere in London in a policeman's uniform. She was glad Bobby was too young to be in a uniform. At least she still had one son at home.

As Maggie and Bella got into the bed they shared together in the attic Maggie said, 'I've never seen so many men in one place'

'All the soldiers liked your piano playing, Maggie. It was so funny to see them all around the piano singing off key. Then when they started singing Polish songs, I didn't understand anything but the tunes were catchy.' Bella yawned, wondered whether Stefan would want to marry her too, closed her eyes and drifted off to sleep dreaming about her handsome Polish soldier.

****

The Lindsays were an extremely close family. All nine of Mrs. Jessie McGregor Mitchell Lindsay's children were constantly competing for her attention, but she always had a kind word for everyone, as a good Christian woman should. She read her Bible every night before she went to bed and had raised her children in the Scottish Presbyterian Church. No one was to come between her and her children, or they would soon get a taste of her fiery Scottish temper. She had once hit a disgusting man with her umbrella when he had exposed himself to her in a dark alley. 'Take that ye dirrty bloke!' She scolded him as she whacked him across the head with it.

Maggie liked Edek's charming ways and invited him to meet her family the following Sunday. 'Come over for tea around five o'clock – I mean – 1700 hundred hours, and I'll introduce you to the rest of my family. Bring your tonsils for a sing-along, as we always have music, and bring your records with you too so that I can let my sisters listen to those romantic tangos.' His big velvety brown eyes intrigued her, but at times they had a hint of sadness.

The day was quite damp with typical Scottish weather Edek and his friends always joked about. 'If you go to the cinema you miss their summer,' laughed Tadek, his roommate in the Nissen hut.

****

Edek was not prepared for what he saw when he walked into Mrs. Lindsay's home. A sliver of dull sunlight was glowing on the brown mahogany table in the sitting room smelling of fresh lemon oil. The windows shone like mirrors creating a glare. There was a jug of dried purple heather in the middle of the table set with white plates. Several woman were sitting near the fireplace talking and laughing with cups of tea on their laps. Bette was sitting by the window shouting to her friends, Maggie came running to meet him wearing a pretty green blouse and a pleated grey skirt. Her hair was tied back with a green ribbon and she looked as fresh as the leaves on the lily of the valley.

'Elizabeth dearie, close that window and don't let the cald air in. We have a guest.' Jessie Lindsay told her youngest daughter while walking forward to meet Maggie's new boyfriend. She had put on her best frock for the occasion.

'This is for your, Mrs. Lindsay.' Edek offered her a package wrapped in brown paper and string, bowing to her.

'I'm pleased to meet you, Edek. Thank you. I wonder what it is?' She smiled putting the parcel on the table to untie it. 'Oh, my goodness! A bottle o' the best brandy.' She exclaimed in delight asking Jess to take it to the kitchen to open it. 'And bring some glasses for everyone. I'm sure Edek would rather have a drap o' brandy than tea.' She smiled at him.

Maggie took him over to the piano, 'This is Jess, Jean and Elsie. You have already met Bella and Bette.' He clicked his heels and bowed to them as if they were royalty. They rose from their chairs to shake his hand.

Jess returned with a tray full of glasses. 'You remind me of - what's-his-name? That film star – oh yes – Laurence Olivier.' She poured brandy for everyone then sat down at the piano and played some Chopin for their honored guest from Poland.

It had been over a year since Edek had any word of his family and he would soon be celebrating another Christmas without them. This cheerful family welcomed him with open arms and he felt an immediate kinship with them which made him miss his family all the more.

'Our Jimmy and George are also in uniform, but wee Bobbie here is too young to be a soldier.' Mrs. Lindsay told him. 'He's a braw laddie, and does all my messages for me.'

'You have a very nice family, Mrs. Lindsay.' Edek said thinking about his own, wondering whether he would ever see them again.

'We go back to Baldric de Lindesaya, a Norman, around 1120, and Sir David Lindsay of Crawford in Angus, around 1398.' Jess, the eldest and best educated of her sisters told him proudly. 'The house of Lindsay established itself in Angus, and we heard that they were always fighting with the Ogilvies and Alexanders. They were always loyal to the Stewarts, and our ancestors supported Mary Queen of Scots. And the Lindsays were also known for their literary talent.' She paused to take a large sip of brandy which went straight to her head.

'You know your history well, Jess. I too, like the subject of history. I studied to be a teacher but when our family ran out of money, I joined the army. Poland also has a very rich history.' He said taking a drink reflecting nostalgically on the past, and wondering silently about the future. They all continued chattering as he listened politely but not understanding everything they were saying as they would often lapse into the Scots dialect. In any case, with six women in the room, he could hardly get a word in.

After supper, they all gathered around the piano again as Jess started playing '*The Bonnets of Bonnie Dundee.*' 'To the lords of convention 'twas Claverhouse spoke...' they all sang as she banged away on the keys while Bobby marched around the house with a broom on his shoulder playing soldier. They all started singing '*Ye Banks and Braes,*' followed by '*There Was a Lad,*' and ending with '*Auld Lang Syne.*'

By now, Edek's bottle of Brandy was nearly empty. 'You are all such a joyful lot, and I really have enjoyed your hospitality, but now I must be going, it is getting close to curfew. Mrs. Lindsay, thank you very much for such a delightful evening, a wonderful supper, and of course, your beautiful daughter.' He smiled broadly.

'It canna be that late! I'm weary too, so I'll be off to my bed soon, and let you run along to yours. Fare thee weel, Edward.' Mrs. Lindsay said putting her knitting in the basket next to the fireplace and covering the bird cage.

Maggie walked her beau to the door shivering in the cold night air, but the warmth of his goodnight kiss soon put a glow on her cheeks.

'Lin, I like your family. Jess plays the piano wonderfully, and I enjoyed hearing Chopin again. Elsie's singing was beautiful. I wish you could meet mine, but they are so far away. Maybe one day soon we can all get together when this war is over.' Edek told her kissing her cheek. Can I see you again next weekend?'

'Yes.' She whispered feeling sorry for him missing his family so much. 'It must be quite sad to be all alone in a foreign country with different customs and having to learn a new language.' She said sweetly.

'I am adjusting, and now that I know you and your nice family, it is much easier. Would you like to see another Hedy Lamarr film? I think next Sunday they are playing '*I Take This Woman*.''

She watched him light a cigarette in the dark hallway. Soon it would be blackout time. She shivered again.

'You are getting cold. Why don't you go in? Shall we meet say - at eighteen hundred - at the cinema?' He took a couple of puffs, then stamped out his cigarette with his shoe. Shall I bring Tadek with me? Do you have a pretty girlfriend for him?'

'My best friend, Jean Ashe, maybe she can come along. Bella is sweet on Stefan.'

'Yes, ask her to come along. Who knows they might like each other. Go inside, my darling, before you catch cold.' He rubbed her arms and held her close one last time.

She waved goodbye rushing inside the house to warm herself at the fireplace. She was freezing on the outside but glowing on the inside.

'I liked your Laurence Olivier.' Jean told her picking up the dishes, joining her other sisters in the kitchen.

Not until she was tucked in bed with Bella in the attic did she realize she would have to buy a new pair of shoes to go dancing, now that she had found a good dancing partner. She decided she would borrow her older sister's black dress to make her look more sophisticated. Her black shoes were a bit scruffy, but they would have to do until she could afford to buy new ones. She decided she would wait to see how Hedy Lamarr had her hair done in the next film, and would copy her style. After all, with a father who was a hairdresser, it would not cost her anything to be fashionable. Oh, to be Hedy! What luck to be in Hollywood! She fell asleep dreaming she was in the arms of Laurence Olivier, because tonight she had been.

The following weekend, Edek and Maggie had tea in the restaurant of the Queen's Hotel, before going to the cinema. Now Maggie was anxious to see a film with Laurence Olivier in it since her sisters were teasing her about Edek's resemblance to him. They decided they would see 'Rebecca' the following week.

Maggie waiting for Edek at the park next to the Queen's Hotel.

Chapter Ten

1940 - The Lindsays

Maggie's father, George Sandeman Lindsay, owned a hairdresser's shop, and managed to feed his nine children by working long hours. His wife, Jessie, worked occasionally as a midwife. Together they formed a very loving family.

Jessie had come from a rich family owners of jute mills, but they had disinherited her because of her independent streak. Her family felt she had married beneath the McGregor name. When she found her happy-go-lucky vaudevillian George, she married him at a young age to escape the control of her interfering older sisters, and never looked back.

Money was not important to her, but family life was her entire world. Their house was always filled with family, friends, music, and laughter. George sang in a barbershop quartet and all the girls learned to play the piano. Those who were singers did not play very well, and those who played well did not sing very well, except for Elsie, she was accomplished in both disciplines.

It was in this fun-loving milieu that Edek felt an immediate kinship with the boisterous Lindsays as they reminded him so much of his own family. How he wished his mother could be around to meet them, but first he had to kick the Nazis out of his homeland. He worried about how they were coping under enemy occupation. Hopefully in the future, when Poland was free, he would take his Lin back to meet them all. In the meantime, there was the damn difficult business of fighting this war they had to win at all costs.

Chapter Eleven

1941 -The Genesis of the 1st Polish Armoured Division

On 07 March 1941, Edek's regiment was ordered to parade in Forfar. General Maczek was arriving to inspect his troops and unveil a plaque. His commanding officers told the men to look sharp as they were now forming the fledgling 1st Armoured Division, which was quickly gaining a good reputation for its efficiency.

Polish commanding officers.   General Maczek
                                         Forfar, Scotland, 1941

Scotts watching a Polish Parade.
Forfar, 07 March1941

Scotts watching a Polish Parade. Edek fifth from right lower
photograph.
Forfar, 07 March 1941

Edek and Tadek were always joking with each
other. Tadek acted more like a comedian than a soldier. 'I
will have to teach you how to kill Nazis. You might run
out of ammunition and have to use your bayonet.' Edek
told him laughing putting his arm around his best friend's
shoulder.

'I'll sharpen it. Don't you worry, you Casanova.'
Tadek replied good-naturedly.

'And who are you going to use it on? A Scotsman?
Uwaga! (Careful!) They keep a knife in their sock if you
get too close to their women they could hurt you.' Edek
slapped him on the back. 'We have to get ready for a

72

parade in a few weeks and you will have to march properly.
Maybe you will catch the eye of a pretty Scottish lass.'
Edek laughed.

'I'll leave the killing to you Edek with your big
tank's gun. You have more of a thirst for blood than I have.
Oh, by the way, were you able to get me that girl, Jean, for
dancing on the weekend?'

'Yes, Lin told me she would come. I can get a lorry
if you can steal some petrol.'

'I have a friend who owes me a favor. I'll take care
of transportation, if you take care of the entertainment!' He
winked, hanging his black leather jacket on a peg over his
cot as he settled in for the night. Damn! These huts were
chilly. He took it down and threw it at the foot of his bed to
cover his cold feet.

Edek's sailor friend was shipping out and sold him
his motorcycle. Now he would be able to travel back and
forth to Dundee to see his beautiful girlfriend and her
wonderful family. By the summer of 1941, life for him
was starting to take on a semblance of normalcy as he was
less than a couple of hours distance from his Lin's Dundee.

Edek's sailor friend sells him the motor bike, Scotland

Maggie watching Edek work odd jobs in the country.

Blairgowrie, Scotland, August, 1941—Soldier's joked with each other 'to whistle while you work so, we know you are not eating the berries'.

Edek was very ambitious and never without extra work.

Labor shortages for agricultural harvests in August in Scotland offered the Poles an opportunity to earn extra money. Edek picked berries and bought Lin presents with his earnings. Soon a cottage industry sprang up in their camps. Edek, being a photo aficionado was never without his Leica camera slung over his shoulder. For despite being a strong character, he was a hopeless romantic, in keeping with the soul of Poland, and finding the Scots equally sentimental.

Ever competitive in sports as in war, Edek broke his left foot playing volleyball. But after it was put in a cast at the Auxiliary Hospital in Dunmore on 21 July, he still wanted to get in the game and played with a broken foot. These young men had an unbridled spirit that the Scots truly admired. It reminded them so much of their own outrageous behavior.

Edek broke his foot playing volleyball

Edek playing volleyball with cast on foot.

****

When the Scottish-Polish Society was formed, Maggie did not hesitate to sign up immediately for Polish language lessons, and having a good ear was able to rapidly pick up a very difficult language. The British Council and many churches also organized social activities such as piano recitals and exhibitions of Polish handiwork. Elsie sang and Maggie played the piano. For despite the war, they were all determined to enjoy life.

It was with planned intent that Germany and Russia had conspired to abolish the spirit of Polish nationalism. What they had not perceived was the true Polish pertinacity, cohesive camaraderie. It was as stubborn as chewing gum on their boots. Impossible to dislodge!

The Nazis hoped to accomplish this by enslaving the Poles, but did not count on their zeal and stubbornness. The Soviets decided they wanted the eastern part of Poland, including Wilno, which Sikorski vehemently objected to. Edek's family's tiny farm in Wolkowysk, near Bialystok on the eastern border of Poland, now found itself deep under Soviet control.

Wolkowysk, Rozany, Poland—Edek's hometown

General Wladyslaw Anders, furious at the treatment the Polish army was receiving at the hands of the Soviets, requested the removal of thousands of Poles out of the Soviet Union and into British controlled Iran, and since the British were needing troops in that area Sikorski grudgingly agreed, knowing that the credit for the defeat of the Germans in Poland would be given to Stalin, thus permitting him the opportunity for dictating the borders and political future of post-war Poland.

This increase in Polish recruits arriving from the Soviet Union enabled the government in exile in London to train the 1st Independent Polish Parachute Brigade in September 1941.

From time to time Edek was able to borrow a lorry to drive to see his sweetheart, and they spent many a happy, sunny afternoon going for long walks in the parks in Duns, Perth, Blairgowrie, and the surrounding Scottish countryside.

Their favourite spot where they could be alone and away from the horrors of war, was in the sunny green landscape filled with pine trees full of nesting black ravens, and various shades of blue and violet from the bluebells and purple heather, and bunny rabbits munching on the tender grass.

One day, on his way to the headquarters of the 1st Polish Corps installed at Moncrieff House near Perth, Edek discovered a lovely bucolic spot called Donald Corgill's Leap, dotted with daffodils and bluebells. He decided it would be a nice place to picnic with his sweetheart.

Edek

Their favourite picnic site
Donald Corgill's Leap near
Blairgowrie.

'Make sure you take your umbrella, because when you plan a picnic outdoors that's when it will surely rain.' Chaim Losize a Polish Jew, who came from Bialystok, billeted with Edek and Tadek said. He was determined to kill as many Nazis as he could. He and Edek had become good friends and their tenacious determination to fight for Poland made them very close comrades.

A weekend in Glasgow, Scotland

The following Saturday afternoon, Edek was able to borrow a lorry and took his Lin for a picnic at Donald Corgill's Leap, the beautiful place dotted with daffodils and bluebells where they could enjoy some fresh air and sunshine. After they had finished eating their ham sandwiches and taking some photos, they had only been there a couple of hours when the slight mist developed into a soft rain. Suddenly a small cloud drifting by turned into a burst of rain that came pouring down drenching them.

Edek hastened to cover his camera as Maggie quickly jumped over the stream, slipped on a lichen-covered rock falling backwards landing on the hard ground narrowly missing the icy water, hurting her back. Unable to walk due to the pain, Edek carried her to the vehicle. Driving as fast as he could in the pouring rain he worried that maybe Lin had fractured her back. He had to get her home as soon as possible and have a doctor examine her.

'What hae ye done tae my lassie?' Mrs. Lindsay shouted in alarm from her window seeing Edek carrying Maggie in his arms who was crying out in pain.

'She hurt her back, Mrs. Lindsay. I think she needs a doctor immediately.' He said placing her gently on the sofa.

'Put her in my bed, and I'll have Bobby run to fetch Dr. Campbell.' Bobby jumped on his bicycle and peddled as fast as his legs would allow.

'I'll go to the kitchen to put on the kettle for hot water for a pot of tea and a hot water bottle. I'll get her some hot compresses for her back, and I'll get her out of those damp clothes before she catches pneumonia.' She said with concern.

'Edek run along and fetch me some aspirin from the chemist shop. She's turned white as snow! Poor lass, she's in terrible pain.' Mrs. Lindsay said wringing her hands in despair.

Dr. Cora Campbell arrived two hours later. 'I am sorry I took so long, Mrs. Lindsay, but I was busy delivering a baby.'

'I'll make you a fresh pot of tea. The rain seems to have slackened off a bit.' She said worried that Maggie might have broken her back as she was wincing in terrible pain.

'I don't think it's broken. You might have a small fracture of the spine, so I would say to take a couple of weeks off work, remain in bed, and refrain from jumping over slippery streams.' Dr. Campbell announced.

While Maggie was indisposed and unable to walk, certainly not able to dance, Edek went with Tadek to see '49th Parallel' with Laurence Olivier. He did not think it would be appropriate to go to the Palais without his girlfriend.

****

June 1941, seemed to be the time for accidents. No sooner did Edek recuperate from his broken foot, now Maggie was unable to dance. He had always been a good athlete, while in Poland he loved to paddle his canoe in the lakes, climb mountains, and ride his bicycle for miles. Maggie was not exactly athletic so their entertainment centered around her piano playing, seeing all the Laurence Olivier films, and picnicking in the countryside near Blairgowrie.

****

The weeks were passing rapidly as Edek continued seeing his sweetheart, but at night in his barracks with Tadek and Chaim, he studied his technical books very seriously.

'What does burnt out bearing mean?' Tadek asked reading the technical dictionary issued to them.

| Technical dictionary issued to the Poles to learn English while training in Scotland. | Inside page of technical dictionary issued to Polish Armoured Division. |

'Let me see your book.' Edek said reaching for it.

At night he was studious about reading his technical books about the armoured vehicles, and had marked this particular problem with a red pen, knowing the answer could save his life someday. He excelled in languages, but also good with mechanics. He remembered watching his father in Poland fix their old car, which was always breaking down. Even though he had studied to become a teacher, anything mechanical also held his interest, and after the war he wanted to return to Poland and maybe open a small camera shop or own a garage and fix cars.

'Edek, put that book down for a minute and tell me whether you were able to get me a girl to go dancing to the Palais again? I am not sure Jean likes me.' Tadek asked enthusiastically.

'I think Lin said she was feeling better, but she would not be able to going dancing. She told me to tell you she had another friend for you and we will all meet at the cinema bar. Can you get transportation? I'm taking Lin next week to see Hedy Lamarr in *'Comrade X.'*'

'If she is as pretty as yours, then yes, but don't saddle me with a fat, ugly woman I am forced to dance with out of politeness.' Tadek shook his head vehemently.

'You must remember, the ugly ones are very grateful.' Edek winked, as they both burst out laughing.

'That's easy for you to say, you attract females like flies to honey, Casanova!' Tadek thought he would stick close to Edek to see if he could attract extra women, and since he was serious with Lin, he would settle for left overs.

'Not to change the subject - but did you hear? Our pilots shot down several *Luftwaffe* planes yesterday.' Edek said seriously.

During the Battle of Britain (*Luftschlacht um England*) from 08 August to 31 October 1940, in the Royal Air Force many enthusiastic Poles distinguished themselves as being aces and shot down hundreds of German planes.

'Yes, I heard we shot down 500 German planes! That's 500 less Nazi's we have to deal with.' Tadek replied, putting on his black leather jacket.

Training was intensifying as more troops arrived daily in Scotland. Some, as far away as Argentina. Edek practiced driving his tank in the hills at Falkanol shooting range.

One Saturday night at the Palais, Edek was completely surprised to see Margaret Lindsay wearing red shoes dancing with a tall, handsome, blonde Norwegian Naval lieutenant commander. He quickly hid behind a curtain to observe them since he could not believe what his eyes were telling him. His Lin was out with another man! His pride would not accept such unfaithfulness. He fumed as he watched her flirting with him. The officer was holding her much too tightly. In disgust, he left early, not even saying goodbye to Tadek who seemed to be chatting along quite nicely with a woman in a uniform at the bar.

The following Sunday, he knocked on Mrs. Lindsay's door and asked to speak to Maggie outside where they quarreled about the incident. He told her in no uncertain terms that he did not expect such behavior from his girlfriend, and decided she was free to see any other man, except him! Maggie ended up in tears and Edek left feeling deceived.

After giving the matter a lot of thought, and with the encouragement of her mother who thought the world of Edek, Maggie took the bus and went to visit him in Duns, to ask his forgiveness wanting to get back together with him. He told her he forgave her but only if she agreed to marry him. They kissed and made up planning a picnic near Blairgowrie.

Chapter Twelve

1941 – 'Larry and Hedy'

On 10 August 1941, Edek borrowed a truck and took Maggie to Donald Corgill's Leap, for a quiet picnic despite the misty day. He needed time to think about the bad news he had just heard about the ill treatment the Polish Army was receiving at the hands of the Soviets in Poland. He felt powerless to help stuck in Scotland. He was upset and unsettled worrying about his family and friends he had left behind in Poland. He desperately wanted to kick the Germans and Russians out of his beloved Poland; but there was not much he could do these days except wait for his chance to fight.

30 August 1941, Donald Corgill's Leap

In November 1941, Edek decided to have another talk with his commanding officer, and this time he would be more insistent. The first time he approached him he was denied permission to get married. But he was madly in love with Margaret Barrie Lindsay, and they wanted to live together. There was too much competition around and he wanted her all to himself.

Driving back and forth to Dundee from Duns where he was billeted was not always easy. Most of the time he rode his motorbike, and for short distances he used his bicycle since petrol was rationed. But when they were having terribly rainy weather he could always manage to get a truck. The best solution was for them to marry and rent a room in a local farmhouse. Lin was working at the post office, but she could find a job elsewhere.

His commanding officer must have been in a romantic mood because this time he granted him permission to marry his Lin.

Mr. and Mrs. Edward Zyrmont, 15 November 1941

Isobel Lindsay, Edek, Maggie, and Tadek Ruta
15 November 1941

Edek on his honeymoon, Alyth

'Tadek, I am going to marry a beautiful Scottish lass with long brown hair and cornflower blue eyes, who plays the piano beautifully.' He exclaimed dancing around the room excitedly.

'Finally, you are going to settle down, you hummingbird! With the trail of broken hearts you have left from Poland to France to Scotland, you will be hiding from their fathers, not German bullets!' He laughed out loud.

All of Edek's friends thought highly of him because he kept a cool head in a crisis, helped them with translations, took photographs of them to give to their girlfriends, could take a joke, was always a gentleman; but it was obvious to everyone that he was head-over heels in love with a girl who looked like Hedy Lamarr.

'Tadek, will you be my best man?'

'I will be honored to be your best man on the happiest day of your life. This calls for a celebration. Call the others.' He reached under his cot and found a bottle of whisky.

Bella was matron of honor and Tadek was best man. Elsie Lawson, Maggie's elder sister made Maggie's warm blue winter dress and the wedding cake. After the civil ceremony they all went over to her house to celebrate the happy occasion.

The Zyrmonts spent their honeymoon in a rented room in Alyth; and a few weeks later moved to another rented room in a house in Blairgowrie.

Blairgowrie, Scotland, March 1941

Edek bought records of Harry James and the Andrew Sisters, but Maggie's favorite was Frank Sinatra singing, '*This Love of Mine,*' with Tommy Dorsey's band. Music always filled their lives whether it was from Maggie playing the piano at her mother's house, or from the music from his records in their room. Edek was constantly whistling or humming the latest tunes, for he was not only a photography aficionado but also a music lover.

****

As the affairs of war maneuvers kept Edek away for weeks at a time practicing moving his tank No. 072, in the hills at Falkanol, Maggie took a rented room in a house in Duns, to be nearer to him. During the week she worked as a telephone operator, and took lessons in the Polish language. She wanted to be able to have a conversational

91

knowledge of it for after the war when she would visit Edek's mother. On the weekends she took the bus back to Dundee to visit her mother and family.

Military funeral in Scotland. A friend was killed in an accident
while on maneuvers, 1942

Sgt. Edward Zyrmont, Tank Commander in his Sherman Tank 072
Duns, May 1942

Chapter Thirteen

1941 - Christmas

On Christmas Eve, Edek took his new wife, the only woman invited to attend the officer's dinner because she spoke a little Polish, to Gibbons Shores in Blairgowrie, where she was introduced to *borscht,* a beetroot soup served with sour cream. Maggie decided to also sign up for Polish cooking lessons as she wanted so very much to please her new husband whom she loved with all her heart. But despite moments of great happiness, no one could really forget the horrors of war they read about in the daily newspapers, and Churchill's constant voice on the wireless.

Officers' Mess, Gibbons Shores, with the Polish Army eating borscht (beetroot soup) on Christmas Day. Maggie was the only woman invited because she now spoke a little Polish. The Poles dislike British food, and fired their British cooks, and used their own Polish soldiers too cook their meals.

June 1942, Fornham Camp, on the outskirts of Bury St. Edmonds with their tanks camouflaged in the trees, at regimental dinner with the President of the Polish Republic, W Raczkiewicz visited their regiment. Edek is second from the right.

By now the Lindsays teased them by calling the newlyweds: 'Larry and Hedy,' knowing of their fondness for seeing films with their favourite film stars. One weekend, Edek took his wife to see Olivier in *'That Hamilton Woman.'*

Sooner than anticipated, there was good news. The Zyrmonts were expecting a child. As the days of her delivery grew closer, Edek did not want to leave his wife alone during his long absences and insisted she move back into Granny Lindsay's house. Not only because she was a midwife, but because he was now going to be away on maneuvers disappearing weeks at a time and felt she was better off with her family in Dundee. It was a very wise decision because Dr. Cora Campbell informed them that the baby would be premature.

Chapter Fourteen

1942 - Daughter of the Regiment

On Easter 1942, Edek arrived at Granny Lindsay's house with a bottle of her favorite brandy, flowers, mince pies and chocolates. It was a boisterous Easter Sunday with the entire Lindsay family.

The happy couple visiting from Duns where Edek was stationed,
29 March 1942

Two weeks later, on 24 April 1942, Dr. Campbell shook her head. 'I am awfully sorry, Mrs. Zyrmont, but I don't think the baby will live through the night. She was born prematurely and her little lungs are not getting enough oxygen. Her lips are blue, which indicates a low blood oxygen, and she is having trouble breathing. I will be back in the morning to take her little body away.' She said sympathetically knowing how much Maggie had wanted this baby. Medical supplies were short and there was nothing much she could do to save the child.

'Ma!' Maggie cried, 'do something! You are a midwife. You have brought many babies into this world. The doctor doesn't know what she is talking about. I can't let her die! Edek will never forgive me if this baby dies. The whole regiment is looking forward to being her godfather.' She frantically tried to blow some air into the baby's mouth. 'Help her!'

'We are not going to let her die! I'll be right back.' Jessie Lindsay told her daughter rushing to the kitchen to get the bottle of brandy that Edek had given her for Easter. She put a tiny bit of brandy on a teaspoon and placed it on the baby's wee tongue. 'This bairn will live, or I'm not Jessica McGregor Lindsay!' She said picking her up and gently patting her on her back, then blowing softly into her mouth. The baby did not respond, so she put another drop of brandy on her tongue further into her mouth and shook her ever so gently.

The newborn made a face, choked, took a deep breath and started crying. Whatever had been stuck in her air passage had now become dislodged with the brandy, and the baby started breathing on its own, crying loudly.

When Doctor Campbell arrived the next morning, she could not believe the nice pink color on the baby's face. 'It's a miracle! I didn't think she would live. She looks as pink as her wee pink blanket. Congratulations Mrs. Zyrmont, you have a beautiful daughter.'

'Would you like a nice cup of tea to celebrate, Dr. Campbell?' Mrs. Lindsay asked very proud of herself wiping her tears with her apron. 'I get paid for my midwife services, so if you ever need one, you know where to find me. After all, I've had nine of my own!' She said pouring a strong cup of tea for the doctor, but in her state of excitement put grated cheese in her teacup thinking it was brown sugar. The doctor made a face, and left in a hurry. The Lindsays were certainly an enigmatic bunch!

After Dr. Campbell left, Granny Lindsay told Bobby to run and take the bus to inform Edek that he had a daughter. Edek rushed back on his motorbike with Bobby in the sidecar, as he only had a couple of free hours from his duties to meet his baby girl.

'We need to find her a very sweet name,' said Wiktor Zolkiewicz.

'My mother's name is Antonina,' Edek said pensively thinking how he would like to tell her she was now a grandmother, but communication was impossible. As soon as he had some free time, he would send her a letter and a photo of his new family, hoping she would get it, but knowing it would be censored.

'No, that is too long,' said Second Lieutenant Czeslaw Morawski.

Dundee Scotland, 24 April 1942. After his Easter visit, Edek had to return to weeks later for the birth of his daughter.

They were all sitting around a wooden table in the field on a warm spring day having a drink to celebrate the good news that now the baby was the daughter of their regiment. 'My sister's name is Helena.' Edek thought out loud.

'But you don't want two Helena's in the family. I have an idea,' shouted Tadek excitedly after his third drink. 'Why don't we all write on a piece of paper our favourite name and put it in Edek's hat. Then let him pick one out, and whatever it is - that will be her name!'

'Whatever her first name is, we have to give her the second name of Maria in honour of the Black Madonna of Czestochowa. We are fighting for Poland and it has been a Roman Catholic country since Mieszko I, in 966 A. D.' Mietek Grebalski chimed in.

'Is that acceptable to you Zyrmont? After all, that is what we are fighting for – the freedom of Polish souls.' Mietek reasoned.

'What is this we?' Edek exclaimed after a stiff drink. 'She's my baby!' He said thumping his chest with pride.

'Edek, have another drink and sit down and pull a name from your hat. It has to be your hat! She is the daughter of our regiment, so pick a nice name.' Mietek laughed pouring everyone another glass, then handed everyone around the table a piece of paper. 'Start writing!' They all threw their papers with their favourite names into his beret.

Edek drank his whisky quickly, closed his eyes, and pulled a piece of paper from his black beret. 'Alicja!' He shouted in amazement. 'Alicja will be her name. Any objections?'

'St. Alicja is the patron saint of the blind.' One of his friends told the group, which by now had finished off two bottles.

'Mietek,' Edek said enthusiastically, 'Will you do me the honour of being her godfather?'

'I will be happy to do so. Then it is decided by all of us. We will baptize her Alicja Maria, at the cathedral in Dundee. She will be the mascot of our regiment. Our little good luck charm.' Mietek said raising his glass. 'Let's toast to Alicja, our little pink Alinka. She will bring us all good luck. She is the first baby to be born into our regiment; our hope for the future.'

'To Catholic Poland and *Matka Boska.*' They all stood up shouting in unison raising their glasses breaking into song: 'Jeszcze Polska Nie Zginela Kiedy My Zyjemy....'

'Well – if we are to remember Catholic Poland and the *Czarna Madonna* (the Black Madonna) we will have to give her a Christian name,' mentioned Wiktor.

'Wiktor, get your nose out of that glass. We have already decided on a name.' Edek laughed heartedly slapping him on the back.

By now there was a crowd of about twenty soldiers who came in to join them when they heard them singing and congregated around the table, not knowing what the loud celebration was all about, but happy to get a glass to raise to Poland. For a brief moment, happiness reigned under the pine trees in the 'laughing barrels.'

'I've got it!' said Henryk coming in from outside. 'You have to call her Maria,' remembering the Matka Boska of Czestochowa, our patron saint.

'Henryk!' Shouted Edek above the din, 'We have already decided she is to be called Alicja Maria.'

On 20 June 1942, Alicja Maria Zyrmont, was baptized in St. Andrews Cathedral in Dundee with Mietek Grebalski standing in as her godfather, and the entire Protestant Lindsay family admiring the stain glass windows. She would represent the future of free Catholic Poland. This little baby brought new hope and joy to the men who would eject the communist atheists from their country. The Poles had no love for the Soviets.

Mietek Grzebalski, Alinka's godfather in Dunns Park, 27 December 1942

Margaret Barrie Lindsay was raised a Presbyterian by her mother a devout Christian, who had the habit of reading her bible every evening by the fireplace with a wee glass o' brandy just to 'Sweeten the words of Jesus,' she would tell her parakeet Joey, before going to bed.

Granny Lindsay found comfort in saying a wee prayer for 'Our poor lads fighting in the war,' remembering the burned lungs from the lads in WW1, just twenty- three years earlier. Joey soon learned to repeat Mrs. Lindsay's favorite passage from the King James Bible, Psalm 23, 'The Lord is my shepherd…' the parakeet would repeat in a squeaky voice greeting folks coming into the sitting room.

Maggie had not told her mother that she was secretly converting to Catholicism to please Edek, and that she had been taking lessons from Sister Veronica, but when the nun committed suicide Maggie was visibly shocked and abandoned the idea completely.

Chapter Fifteen

Wings of Hussars

Finally, and with great anticipation, in February 1942, the Polish 1st Armoured Division was operational with 16,000 soldiers. Everywhere in villages and towns around Scotland, the Polish language could be heard. Cars had PL marked on them to denote they belonged to the Polish Division. Sometimes tanks found their way onto narrow roads with buses and lorries having to give way to them. Soon, recognition badges appeared on their vehicles.

The insignia proudly worn on the shoulders of soldiers of the 1st Armoured Division, was designed by Captain Stanislaw Glaser, his drawing consisted of 'wings' worn by soldiers of the 'armoured cavalry' in ancient Poland, combined with a helmet against an orange circle piped with black; the colours of the Polish Armour. Thus this Armoured Division was linked in history with the Polish heavy cavalry regiments, denoting the wings of the famous Hussars, and which was approved by the War Secretary on 11 August 1942, as their badge of honour.

Two hundred and sixty years before the Hussars had fought off the might of Turkey and saved the Christian city of Vienna from destruction. Sienkiewicz famously described such a charge in the battle of Zbaraz: 'The regiments rode up as though they had wings, their standards fluttering, the wind whistling through their feathers....'

Since Scottish soil was unfit for tanks with its hills, gorges, valleys, and interspersed with streams, the tank drivers preferred to drive on the roads instead. Farmers and locals hastily jumped out of their way as the errant tanks tended to smash into walls, fences and telephone poles. Many a farmer could be seen shaking his fist at them: 'Bloody Pole! I'll nae hae any sheep left if ye canna learn to drrive these tanks without crashing into my walls!'

Duns Scotland, 1942

Polish could be heard spoken in Duns, Kelso, and Galashiels. Some soldiers were being trained in Bovington and Lulworth on the coast of Dorsetshire in Southern England, as they struggled to learn English from the technical dictionaries about vehicles and tanks.

Dunns, Berwickshire, 1942

Chapter Sixteen

1943 - The 1st Polish Armoured Division

The 1st Polish Armoured Division was organized in Duns, Scotland. On 04 July 1943, Wladyslaw Eugeniusz Sikorski, the Prime Minister of the Polish Government in Exile, and Commander-in-Chief of the Polish Armed Forces, and a vigorous advocate of the Polish cause, was killed in an airplane crash after immediate takeoff from Gibraltar under mysterious circumstances. Sikorski had requested that the International Red Cross investigate the Katyn Forest massacre, and also supported the reestablishment of diplomatic relations between Poland and the Soviet Union. Many soldiers in Edward Zyrmont's Division were strongly opposed to Stalin. His successor, General Sosnkowski, reorganized the Division, but it was still short about 3,150 soldiers, and Montgomery would not authorize them for fighting, causing them to mistrust him.

A series of successes of Allied armies in the East and the West originated the Stalingrad victory, which was a serious setback for the Third Reich. Russian armies crossed the Dnieper River, Anglo-American troops landed in Italy. Western Allies began to organize the Second Front on a large scale, which emboldened the Poles living peacefully in Scotland; however, they were desperate to get back into the fighting. They had met General Eisenhower, the Supreme Commander of the invasion armies, and unlike Montgomery, they trusted him. His headquarters were at Bushy Park near Kingston on Thames.

Despite politics, 1943 was a happy year for the hopeful Poles as Edek trained constantly with his tanks in the Scottish countryside, and with typical Polish pertinacity, he studied hard to learn all about the construction of his tank engine, the driving system, the hydraulic operation, and many other secrets of the steel giant he would soon command.

Maggie settled into domesticity raising Alinka while working. She paid two old spinsters, Fiona and Moira, in Duns to look after the baby while she worked as a telephone operator in a nearby office. She was issued a certificate of registration as the wife of a Polish officer, and now became entitled to certain privileges such as seeing the military dentist and extra rationing.

Maggie enjoyed her life while Edek continued working extra jobs to make money for his new family. The summer harvest of 1943 with the farmers in Berwickshire was over, but Edek found odd jobs in carpentry and photography. Edek was always scheming of ways to make extra money, as he was one of the most ambitious soldiers in his unit.

Sundays were always family outings with Mietek and Tadek enjoying playing with the baby while Edek took photos incessantly. Little Alinka got a lot of attention from the men since she was the mascot of their brigade as she represented an innocence in a world of destruction.

Edek with his daughter, Alicja Maria in Duns Park, 1942

Maggie and Alinka, Duns, 1942

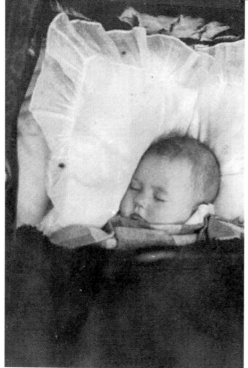

September 1942, Duns

Dundee Scotland, 23 June 1942

Maggie sent food supplies and an army blanket through the Red Cross to Edek's family in Poland, but she could not be certain whether they had received the gifts, as there was never an answer. One of the photos she had sent to his mother, Antonina, was a picture of herself standing with Edek seated holding Alinka on his knee. Again, there was no reply.

Dundee, Scotland 1942 Edek sent this photograph through the
British Red Cross to his mother in Poland, and she had it enlarged to
6 feet, pasted on a cardboard and stored in closet.

Chapter Seventeen

1943 - The Second Wedding

Caught up in his best friend's happiness, Mietek Grzebalski, also decided to marry his sweetheart, Henrietta Darling Murray, on 02 February 1943 in Galashiels, so there was cause for a big celebration. Another excuse for some happy moments and bottles of whisky. After all, life was to be lived to the fullest!

Mietek Grzebalski, married in Galashiels
02 March 1943

1943 continued to be a good year for the soldiers, which as far as Maczek was concerned, were setting the finest of military standards, and he was extremely proud of his *1 Polskiej Dywizji Pancernej. (First Polish Armoured Division.)*

Edek was now beginning to spend longer days away from his family while on maneuvers around Scotland, but kept in touch writing to his Lin every free moment he got. She cherished his letters and kept them tied up with a green ribbon in a box of Players' cigarettes.

'Darling,

Work keeps me very busy these days as I learn all about the mechanics of my tank. I am not allowed to tell you much about my work here, as I told you, they do censor our mail, but I take this moment to tell you how much I miss you both.

I can smell the heather in your hair, I look up at the blue skies, and see your blue eyes. I think of your laughter and your piano playing, and all the films we saw together, and I just want to rush to your side. I would love to embrace you and kiss my sweet baby girl, but for now, all I can do is dream about you.

Take good care of yourself.

Your loving husband,

Edek'

His letters came frequently, and were a great source of comfort to her.

'My dearest Lin,

I only have a few free minutes to write to you, so I wanted you to know that I love you with all my Polish heart. I think about you and Alinka every night and pretend you are beside me. I have your photo pinned over my bunk. I must rush to post this letter. With all my love, give a big kiss to the baby. I sent you a present. I hope you like it.

Your dearest,

Edek'

'My love, my angel,

It has been weeks since we have been separated and I miss you so much. A dull grey sky surrounds us today. As you know, our letters are censored, so I can't tell you where we are, but these long miles of separation are as bad as a thousand nights of being without you in this cold. My only consolation is knowing you love me. With a heavy heart, I say goodbye for now as I am running out of ink. I close by telling you this separation for me is an endless heartache. Goodbye my angel, my darling Lin – no not goodbye – 'till we meet again' as the song goes. I want you for all the days, no, years, no, all eternity to come.

Your

Edek'

'My lovely lass, Lin,

I am writing in red ink because that is all I have, but it is the color of my passion for you, as we have no more supplies, but I wanted to get this letter off to you, and I would write in pencil if that is all I had, and if no pencil, then I would send you a note with a carrier pigeon, I would whistle a tune, hope he could memorize it and repeat it to you when he sees you. It would say, 'I love you. I miss you. I need you.' Your lonely husband,

Edek'

'Dearest Mrs. Zyrmont,

I am happy to write that I should soon be home on leave. I send all my good thoughts and love to you. How is Alinka growing? Is Fiona still knitting pink cardigans for her? Tell her thanks so much, and I will bring her a present as my gratitude for being such a wonderful auntie to my baby daughter. I close my eyes at night and wonder what you are doing, and I think of all the beautiful memories we shared together. I count the hours that I will be with you both again. No – I count the minutes.

I love, love, love you,

Edek'

Chapter Eighteen

Hollywood Films

Edek's Division, now reorganized was getting ready to move to Aldershot. The soldiers were anxious to be part of the landings in France. Edek was itching to kill some more Germans. He wanted to fight now, not when the damn war was over. He had trained intensely to get at the Nazis, and if there were some Ruskis around, that would be even better. The Russians could not be trusted to leave their beloved homeland alone.

Back on leave, one summer evening, just to forget about the problems and rationing of war, Edek invited his Lin to see a film: '*Hello, Frisco, Hello*', starring Alice Faye. She sang a song that Maggie could not get out of her mind: '*You'll Never Know.*' She asked her sister to buy the sheet music so that she could play it on the piano. Maggie would watch Jess play the piano and studied her finger work. In no time at all she had mastered the sentimental song and played it for Edek while he sang the lyrics. He had a lovely baritone voice and together they would spend hours at Granny Lindsay's house entertaining themselves singing. The family agreed, it was definitely their song. And when Vera Lynn sang it on the wireless she ran out and bought the record.

For them, American films meant a couple of hours escaping into a fantasy land full of beautiful music, glamour, and a short relief from the ugliness of war.

Maggie told him that when the war was over she wanted to go to California.

'But what happened to Argentina? You wanted to go there to learn to dance the tango. Suddenly you want to visit California. I was thinking of returning to Poland after the war. We shall see, my darling. We shall see.' He said in a melancholy tone.

Chapter Nineteen

1943 – *Burza*! Operation Tempest!

In 1943, Gen. Sikorski, the prime minister in exile, had secured the release of portions of the two million civilian and military Poles who had been deported to Soviet labor camps in 1939. They traveled through the Middle East, and were eager to fight when they arrived in Britain, but were in no physical condition for rigorous training. When Sikorski was killed in an airplane accident, Poland was left without a strong leader to represent her at a time when the demands of a coalition warfare were important.

Sikorski had been hopeful that Churchill and Roosevelt could help him come to a favorable agreement for Poland with Stalin, which would permit his government to hold power in Poland with the help of the Polish résistance at the end of the war. But these hopes were dashed when he was killed on 04 July 1943, in a mysterious plane crash at the moment of take-off at Gibraltar.

This left his successor, General Kazimierz Sosnkowski, who was appointed commander in chief, with a dilemma, who believed that the government must defend territorial and political integrity in Poland, despite what the allies thought; as he would not tolerate the 'Sovietisation' of Poland.

The Poles were devastated when at the November Tehran Conference it was left out of the Western Allie's plans for the summer invasion of Europe.

Moments of brief happiness were intertwined with dark moments of despair for Edward Zyrmont. On 05 October 1943, Anthony Eden, the British Foreign Secretary, told the British War Cabinet that it should not supply the Polish Home Army with arms because it would anger the Russians. In accordance with the British government's policy regarding the advancing Soviet forces, it was determined that if Soviet-Polish relations were not restored at the time the Soviets entered Poland, the Home Army should only act behind the German lines, and remain underground.

This decision to conceal the Home Army was dangerous because it might lead to war with the Soviet security forces. The sabotage diversion was intended to be a political demonstration, but if the Soviet Union entered Poland, it would have to be carried out as a clandestine operation with units which had been involved in fighting the Germans going underground again.

General Bor-Komorowski, in the Home Army, received these unrealistic orders and decided to ignore them. He ordered his men engaged in action in February 1944 in Volhynia and Wilno, with the Germans to reveal themselves to the Soviets and 'manifest the existence of Poland.' Some of the local Home Army units would be mobilized and thrown into battle against the Germans. He was afraid that otherwise the Home Army's operations against the Germans would be credited to the Soviet communists. During the fighting temporary contact and some cooperation with the Russians occurred, and some relations were relatively friendly. After the fighting, those of the Home Army units found themselves in Russian-held territory, and would be disarmed, then incorporated into the Russian army, or deported to Russian camps.

The Polish Home Army had to wait for the German retreat then launch a general and simultaneous insurrection: *Burza*; a simple plan. It was to begin in the east and move westwards as military operations moved into Poland. It was to be a number of consecutive uprisings started in different areas as the Germans retreated. As *Burza* continued it became clear that Stalin did not want to cooperate militarily or politically with Poland.

No operations were to be taken against the Soviet forces, or the Polish Army raised in the USSR. The success of *Burza* was dependent upon good timing. Premature engagement with the Germans unassisted by the Red Army could turn Polish attacks into disasters.

Initially, big cities were to be excluded from *Burza* in order to spare the population from suffering, so a delay was ordered.

The early months of 1944, passed rapidly as Edek was extremely busy with training affairs and spent more weeks away from his love nest. Maggie noticed that he had become more morose and silent. She sensed something ominous was developing, but he would not talk about it. She knew he would be returning to France because he had been issued French francs. It was obvious to her that he would be shipped off to France once again as rumours of an imminent invasion were whispered in churches.

'Are you going to fight in France again?' She asked nervously, not really wanting to hear his answer.

'You know I can't talk about it. There are rumours sweetheart, but as they say, 'loose lips sink ships.' They tell us nothing.' He said shaking his head wanting to change the subject.

'But Edek, I need to know where you are? How can I write to you? What will I tell your mother – I'll have to write her a letter in broken Polish, with the help of...' she trailed off in tears.

He interrupted her and held her gently by the shoulders: 'No! You must not do that! Nobody knows for certain where we are going; or when. In any case, she might not get your letter, and it would be intercepted. For now, there can be no contact. Promise me, Lin, you will not write to her.'

Maggie sat sadly watching him pack his belongings. 'I am leaving tomorrow on a transport train, and I suspect we are leaving for France. If I know for certain, I will send you a postcard saying I am going to visit Mrs. Apolinarski. Remember, my old war mother. That will be our code. Then you will know that is where I will be fighting. But you cannot tell anyone, not even your family. Promise me.'

'I will come to see you off…' her voice cracked as she watched him go over to the crib, pick up his sleeping baby and place a kiss on her forehead. For her husband's sake she tried to be brave and not break down; not until he was gone. As the heaviness in her heart would have to be repressed into her consciousness for a long time.

'My dear Lin, you will never find me in thousands of uniforms at the station. Please don't come to the station. Let's say goodbye here.'

Tears swelled up in her blue eyes. She clung to him with love and stoicism, then irresolutely watched him open the door to leave on a warm summer day that brought a chill to her very soul. She would never forget that moment as long as she lived. It seared itself into her memory causing a heartbreak she never knew existed in her young life.

Edward Zyrmont embraced and kissed his wife tenderly one last time, but now his heart turned to stone. He would become a warrior again. It was time for retribution to rid the murderers from his country for good. He had waited for over four long years for the opportunity to kill them, to rid Europe of the genocide of the Third Reich, and the terrible atrocities they were committing. They would soon learn what the Black Devils of the 1st Polish Armoured Division were made of.

****

In September 1944, the exiled Polish government in London dismissed Sosnkowski due to his absolute refusal to support a reconciliation with the Soviets, which was highly encouraged by the British government. But he believed that this now became a 'Problem for the conscience of the world, and a test case for the future of European nations.'

During this time, there was very little sympathy between the British government and the Polish government in exile. Yet the Poles were a tightly loyal unbreakable group. When they met General Eisenhower, they were impressed with his honesty, and the division was more than ready to move to Portsmouth awaiting their return to meet the Germans once more in France.

Even though his time in Scotland had been heaven on earth, Edek was very eager to give the Nazis a taste of their own medicine. He had bided his time for years, but he had never forgotten what they had done to his country, his beloved Poland, and to his dear family, or the defeat they received by the Nazis in Poland and France. He would kill as many of the bastards as was humanly possible!

When Edek got onto his motorbike, the sound of his roaring engine deafened Maggie as she slumped in the armchair by the fireplace in a state of shock, unable to cry, staring at her baby daughter in her little pink outfit Fiona had knitted. She would have to compose herself and reach to the bottom of her strength to continue with her life and work for the baby's sake, wondering how her husband's personal revenge would go yet feeling a despair knowing he would never come back.

How strange to have a large invasion that would change her life forever, yet not knowing anything about it. She felt as if she were in a world of fantasy, in a Hollywood film, where reality blended with make believe. She felt totally out of her body. She was living a drama she had not asked for. She was simply stunned, unable to comprehend the magnitude of the moment. Lost in emotions she had never experienced before. She left the crying baby with Fiona, and walked into town.

It was eerily quiet, deserted. Even the farmers were standing at the side of the road like clay statues to say their final goodbyes to their guests, it was as if everything had suddenly turned into slow motion. One collective breath had been taken in and not let out, but when it did, it would be one terrible roar. A roar of death that the world had not heard since WWI.

Maggie had never heard such an earth shattering silence, not even in church. Many women had gone into church knowing there would be a catastrophe, not daring to say a word about it to each other, but everyone instinctively knew about the invasion. Maggie wished she was in her mother's house as she had always been such a source of great comfort to her, but she was miles away and she would have to wait until the weekend to visit her.

The following morning, Maggie wrapped the baby in a pink shawl, and went over to Chrissy Velaney's house, and the two women married to Polish soldiers, stone-faced boarded a train to Tilbury, in the hopes of seeing their husbands for the last time. Neither one of them had enough money for a ticket. When the conductor asked them for their tickets, Maggie buried her face in the baby's shawl crying, 'We are on our way to see our husbands off to war, but we don't have the money for the fare.'

Noting their distress, the conductor said, 'Never you mind lassies, it is my gift to you, since you are giving the gift of your husbands to the war effort, I'll not report you.'

At the station, Maggie stood up on a wooden bench while Chrissy cradled her sleeping baby. After about ten minutes, she could not believe her good luck. She spotted him in a sea of uniforms. 'Edek!' She yelled waving excitedly, 'Edek!'

Her husband pushed his way through the crowd of soldiers to reach his wife, flinging his arms around her despite his kitbag. He held the world in his arms while Maggie clung to him with a longing she never knew existed. She smiled and cried simultaneously. He picked the baby up and kissed her little fat cheeks. They only had a few minutes to say another goodbye, but it felt like an eternity. She wanted him to remember her smiling though her heart was broken. Chrissy found her husband too, they only had seconds to hug and kiss and said their last goodbye. The women watched the train leave and felt they were taking a part of their lives with them.

On their return trip to Dundee, Maggie sat motionless as tears streamed down her pale face. She knew instinctively she would never see her beloved Edek again and felt a hollow where her heart should be. She buried her face in her handkerchief blowing her nose, staring out the window all the way home in a trance unable to say one single word to Chrissy. If the conductor came by and called the police because they did not have tickets, she was totally oblivious. She was not in this world! But the carriage was empty as empty as her soul.

General Bernard Montgomery Commander of all Allied Ground Forces, during Operation Overlord. General Montgomery addressing Polish troops.

General Guy Simods, II Candian Corps

General Dwight David Eisenhower, Supreme Commander of
Allied Forces, Europe, addressing Polish Troops.

Chapter Twenty-one

06 June, 1944 – D-DAY!

Operation OVERLORD had begun!

General Dwight D. Eisenhower, was the supreme commander of the Allied Forces in Europe. In his headquarters near Portsmouth, he planned to invade France on 05 June 1944, but he hesitated when the weather began to deteriorate. The troops proceeding to the ports were halted. Later, a meteorological report arrived to be more favorable, and Eisenhower decided no further postponement would be necessary.

By the end of July 1944, the Polish 1st Armoured Division with 1800 men, two tank regiments and three infantry battalions, crossed the Channel from Tilbury, England, to Normandy, arriving at the artificial Mulberry Harbour near Arromanches, on August 1, 1944. It was attached to the First Canadian Army, as part of the 21st Army Group, under the command of Lieutenant General Guy Simonds, Second Canadian Corps. General Bernard L. Montgomery was placed in command of Operation Totalize.

On 08 August 1944, Lt. Gen. Omar Bradley, commander of the American First Army, called Gen. Montgomery and informed him that it would be a great opportunity if the bulk of the American Twelfth Army Group were to push eastward along the German's southern boundary while other U. S. divisions kept the Germans fighting along its perimeter, and then turn northward at Argentan to meet the Canadians heading south through Falaise, and could encircle and 'destroy an entire hostile army.' Gen. Montgomery thought it was a good plan.

However, this difficult plan depended entirely on the Canadians being able to break through German lines north of Falaise. Under Lt. Gen. Sir Henry Crerar, whom Montgomery disliked, the Canadians had already launched an attack, on 07 August.

Gen. Simond's II Canadian Corps, moved out of their cover of darkness, but lost their way due to heavy Allied artillery and aerial bombardment, and encountered the Germans who fought savagely. But the Canadians had some success and were breaking through the German lines when due to bad visibility RAF bombers miscalculated and dropped some bombs on the 4th Canadian Division, and the 1st Polish Armoured Division, killing 65 soldiers.

The Polish army was ordered to go south toward Caen to join up with the Canadians and Americans, and attack the German lines at Falaise. Having failed to reach Falaise, 'Totalize,' was stopped, but with the operation of the Second Canadian Corps, 'Tactable,' made it possible for the 1st Polish Armoured Division to spearhead a breakthrough, however, not without grave difficulties and at a terrible price. Their first encounter with the Germans occurred during Operation Totalize, on 08 August, 1944, southeast of Caen.

On 09 August, the Poles distinguished themselves in the battle for Renemesnil, receiving very heavy artillery and mortar fire near a church, yet managed to reach the western outlets of Cauvicourt. The 1st Armoured Regiment had been able to break the German defences near the Laison River and reach Hill 111, and proceeded to attack it, but not without cost of many wounded. However, it did accomplish freeing about 100 Canadian soldiers who had been without supplies for two days, thus able to greatly demoralize the German infantry garrison.

On 15August, it crossed the Dives River near Jort, and reconnoitered near the woods of Courcy. On 18 August it was ordered to attack in the direction of Bourdon to enable the resupply of Lt. Col. Koszutski's group. However, that was an impossible task as the Allied Air Force mistakenly bombed them thinking they were enemy tanks.

By 19 August, they were able to control the area of Coudehard, despite being heavily engaged with Panzer tanks and under heavy enemy fire. By night fall the 1st Armoured Regiment, 1st Mountain Rifle Battalion, and one anti-tank battery occupied both Hills 262 and 252, which Maczek called: 'Maczuga.'

Chapter Twenty-two

1944 – The Falaise Gap: 'Maczuga'

The 1st Canadian Army had incorporated the 7th British Armoured Division, and the 1st Polish Armoured Division, under the command of Lt. General Sir Henry Crerar. General Maczek, following the principles of tactics, advised General Simonds, a young and temperamental Canadian, not to attack Trun frontally, but first master the dense woody hills east of Trun and Chambois.

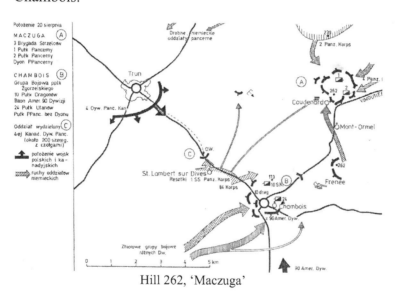

Hill 262, 'Maczuga'

The Polish rear echelon detachment completely encircled by Germans found itself in a dangerous situation. They were not in the area they were supposed to be. The radios went out of action, and the US Eighth Air Force, with about 20 American Thunderbolts flying overhead accidentally bombed them, killing over 60 men and wounding 300, destroying large amounts of their ammunition.

Hawker Typhoons of No. 198 Squadron from the Royal Air Force, decimated a retreating armoured column of the German Seventh Army, at Falaise, because of poor visibility.

Another problem they found was that the Sherman tanks were outgunned and the Germans had faster and better armoured tanks manned by veteran crews. Now reorganizing into two columns to meet up with the Americans, the Polish Division progressed towards Chambois.

It was the 2nd Canadian Corps 'Tractable' which made it possible for them to finally break through. With supporting Dragoons and anti-tank guns, they advanced on 15 August towards the Dives River. They had been ordered to travel south-east towards Caen, but they soon got lost. Their French guide had misunderstood their thick Polish accent and on the 18 August, instead of sending them to Chambois, to join the Americans, he mislead Lieutenant Colonel Stanislaw Koszjutski on a false trail to Champeaux, 20 kilometers away inside enemy territory.

'Cholera! Cholera!' The commander swore profusely in Polish, ordering all the tank commanders to encircle him while he read the map. 'We are in Les Champeux, which is about 20 kilometers from Chambois. We missed our target! Bloody hell!' And we are right behind the German positions!' Shouted Lieutenant Colonel Nowaczynski.

The French guide mysteriously disappeared.

Edward Zyrmont was a tank commander in the C, 3rd Squadron. The Poles moved their tanks by night into unknown wilderness. It was extremely dark in the woods, and this did not help them to find their way. Soon the advanced guard ended up in a highway at a crossroad right into the German Second Panzer SS Division column. He shouted: 'there is a German column right in front of me!' Lieutenant Colonel Koszutski kept calm and ordered: 'Don't break formation. Don't shoot. Move!' Counting on the surprise astonishment of the German traffic controller, who halted the flow of his tanks, then noticed they were actually Poles, he pretended not to recognize them in order to avoid a total disastrous close-range encounter; and then unbelievably let them pass!

'Cholera! Pieklo na ziemi!' The Polish soldier in the first tank said thinking it was going to be the end of his days, wiping his forehead with a dusty glove, afraid to look back in case the Germans changed their minds and started shooting.

The Falaise pocket was an area between Trun, Argentan, Vimoutiers, Chambois, near Falaise, in which the Allied forces encircled to destroy the German Seventh Army and their Fifth Panzer Army.

The 1st Division turned towards the east and after three days of heavy fighting, on the 19 August captured two areas. These two hills were 262, 'the Club' and Chambois. Now they were ordered to hold, but the 2nd SS-Panzer Korps managed to open a breach but could not get through Stefanowicz's task force.

The Germans were eager to escape their fate and break through. The 2nd Armoured Regiment was ordered to join the main divisional forces. Some in the regiment were able to reach the Rouvre River, they were unable to break through the deep German defensive system. They failed to reach Falaise, and 'Totalize' was halted, but for days they fought their way out of the *bocage* moving agonizingly slow.

The Poles were ordered to stand ground on Hill 262, they called, 'Maczuga.' The Germans were attempting to escape from the ring of allied divisions surrounding them, as they had heard the invasion had started, and the Americans were at their rear. But counter-attacks by the Nazis continued endangering the Polish defence line.

On 19 August, 1944, the rain turned into a downpour and all during the next day, hampering Allied artillery observers. Hill 262, on Mont Ormel ridge, the 'Mace' as Maczek referred to it, the 2nd SS-Panzer Korps, under the command of General von Kleist, managed to break through but could not get free of Major Aleksander Stefanowicz's task force.

On the morning of 20 August, the Poles saw the plain full of Germans in vehicles and on foot, and long columns of transport driving in an orderly fashion towards the northeast. They started firing down on the Germans below with everything they had as the Nazis ran for cover, but the Poles quickly became short of ammunition. From their high vantage point on the hill, they were able to direct artillery on the retreating Nazis exacting a vicious toll on them, finally able to get their long-awaited revenge, but running short of bullets. The Poles let them have it, but the Germans tried to keep their escape routes open, with two Panzer Divisions, which had crossed the Seine to the west bank and proceeded towards Mont Ormel.

They also ran out of food, water, petrol, and medical supplies. They desperately needed support from the 2nd Canadian Armoured Division, but Colonel de Langlade's armoured group, and the 90th US Division were heavily engaged in fighting at Chambois. Supplies could only be brought in by air from England. Unfortunately, due to bad weather and poor visibility because of high winds, low clouds and heavy rain the sorely needed containers were dropped five kilometers short and fell into enemy hands.

For two days and nights they fought completely cut off from supplies and without the possibility of evacuating their wounded. It was then that Polish soldiers showed their valour, fortitude, and will to fight to their deaths. They withstood fierce attacks from the German best divisions, such as the First SS Panzer Division: the 'Adolf Hitler,' and the Twelfth SS Division 'Hitlerjugend.'

This Polish Division fought with all its strength. The battlefield was covered with hundreds of dead bodies and damaged equipment, but they managed to capture an escaping Nazi General, Commander of the Eighty-fourth Corps, General Elfeldt, and his staff.

By now the road from Chambois to Vimoutiers was completely filled with escaping German troops, totally congested with burned-out vehicles, bloated dead corpses, and exhausted soldiers making their way from the Dives Valley towards Germany, which became a congested corridor of death. The Germans worked feverishly to escape, but first had to clear the wreckage of vehicles careening through fields, crazed neighing of wounded horses, dodging the whining howls of bullets, shrieks of wounded men, vehicles on fire, dust and smoke, the sharp cracks of rifles, lorries crashing and burning, smashed artillery pieces, wagons, tanks, guns, and men in various stages of destruction. The killing was everywhere as flies and maggots descended on bodies decaying in the hot August sun. It was Dante's Inferno reincarnate.

The Poles continued fighting the enemy with a passion and zeal from pent up frustration as they were determined to kill as many Nazis as they could. This was their opportunity for retaliation. They had waited a long time for this moment, and revenge was sweet. Out of bullets, Corporal Lukasik shouted 'Fix bayonets!' and hand-to-hand combat, as they had been trained to do in Scotland, began in earnest. To add to this chaos, the Poles had hundreds of German prisoners with ragged uniforms to attend. When three German officers surrendered saluting saying, '*Heil Hitler!*' Major Stefanowicz reached for his revolver. It would be so easy to shoot the bastards in cold blood, but his conscience as a Catholic dictated that he never wanted to become an animal like them, and instead gave an order: 'Kosakowski, take them away!'

Under an apple tree, a makeshift hospital tent was very busy with hundreds of wounded. 2nd Lieutenant Szygowski, a medical officer of the 9th Battalion worked to the point of exhaustion. Across the field was a small farmhouse which had been converted into a field hospital. Someone shouted: 'Panzers!' The Germans drove on firing shots on the medical personnel without regard to the Red Cross on a white flag on the tent surrounded by ambulances. Bullets hit the tent housing the wounded in a continuous shower as Corporal Noras desperately waived a white flag with the Red Cross on it attempting to show that there were also wounded Germans in it, but a bullet hit him in the head killing him instantly.

A truce was called for twenty minutes to enable both sides to pick up their wounded, as a nauseating smell of burning flesh permeated the hill. Then the fighting resumed with more violence than ever in a special hell the Poles had reserved for the Nazis. It was payback time for what they had done to their homeland: for the rape of their sisters, the enslavement of their families, the destruction of their beloved country. They would not stop firing on the retreating Germans, and the fight continued well into the evening.

The two Polish regiment commanders, Koszutski and Stefanowicz, met to discuss the seriousness of the situation. They were cut off with their 80 tanks behind German lines. As the Polish machine guns from their vantage point on the hill slaughtered Nazis below, and they were full of zeal for revenge for the massacre they had suffered years before at the Bzura River, they both understood their victory could not last long with their dwindling supplies and the hundreds of surrendering German soldiers.

On 20 August, the Poles were caught in a crossfire of a counter-attack by the 21st Panzer Division, units of the *Das Reich's* SS *Armoured Division,* retreating on their way towards the outside of the gap from Vimoutiers.

Koszutski ordered five Shermans to engage them, but seeing them surrounded, quickly changed his mind. Too late! Sgt. Edward Zyrmont, following orders eager to attack the approaching Panzers, stood up in his tank waiting for the thick smoke to clear, looking through his field glasses unable to see clearly to direct his gun on them. This was his moment; his courage came from rage, from a sense of revenge for what the Nazi scourge had done to his beloved homeland.

The Panzers moved quietly under cover of thick bushes and were 1600 meters away when suddenly out of nowhere they opened an unforgiving barrage of shellfire at the five Sherman tanks sent out to find them. Within a matter of seconds they had set on fire the tanks with their 88 mm guns killing the troop commander, Second Lieutenant Adamczewski, and tank commander Sergeant Zyrmont. Two of his men scrambled out of the burning tank pulling Zyrmont out, but both his legs had been blown off. He died immediately.

For Sergeant Edward Zyrmont, a ten-year veteran in the Polish Army, the war was over! But he died knowing they were achieving victory over the Wehrmacht.

The 3rd. Squadron escaped towards the clearing to avoid the same fate. With their 75 mm guns they were powerless to strike back at such range. Artillery barrages rained down as mortars kept flying overhead as Polish soldiers dived headfirst into trenches. In the distance the 21st German Armoured Division moved up from the west to crush units which were attempting to close the gap, as the Germans hammered the Poles caught in a trap. They came up by the rear and broke the group of Polish units still superhumanly defending the 'Mace.'

The Poles were in a desperate situation sending alarming messages for help. But the nearest support was the Canadian 4th Armoured Division, who were also bogged down in battle and quite mauled, who could not arrive in time to assist. General Simmonds, watched helplessly through his field glasses unable to help the dying Poles.

By nightfall, the Poles were battle fatigued and some laid down next to their tanks and fell asleep. Lieutenant Tedeusz Wielogorski woke up several hours later to find a German sleeping next to him. He had come by in the dark to surrender and meeting no Poles in the bushes, afraid to speak German for fear of being shot, he decided to sit down by the commander of the squadron and fell asleep too. Despite being isolated and coming under further strong attacks the Poles miraculously held on to Hill 262.

Exasperated by the losses of his men, Colonel General Paul Hausser, commanding the Seventh Army, ordered that the Polish positions be 'eliminated.' Substantial forces, including the remnants of the 352nd Infantry Division, and several battle groups from the 2nd. SS Panzer Division, inflicted heavy casualties on the 8, 9, Battalions of the Polish 1st Armoured Division, but the assault was eventually beaten off. Their stand cost the Poles almost all of their ammunition, and left them in a precarious position; lacking the means to intervene, they were forced to watch as the remnants of the XLVII Panzercorps escaped the pocket on its way back to Germany.

After the brutality of the day's combat, nightfall was welcomed by both sides. With contact being avoided, fighting during the night was sporadic, although the Poles continued to call down frequent artillery strikes to disrupt the ongoing German retreat.

Koszutski wounded called his men to his bedside, 'All is lost. I do not think the Canadians can rescue us in time. We have no food, and very little ammunition left, but fight all the same. There is no question of surrender. Tonight we die for Poland and civilization. We will fight to the last platoon, the last tank, then to the last man. Good luck gentlemen.'

German attacks resumed the next morning, and the Poles took further casualties and some were taken prison yet they managed to retain their foothold on the hill. At approximately 11:00A.M., a final attempt on the positions of the 9th Battalion was launched by nearby SS remnants which was defeated at close quarters.

The battle lasted throughout the entire day of the 21st. On the late afternoon of 21 August, the first armoured units of the 4th Canadian Armoured Division, finally succeeded in linking up with the besieged Polish forces at Coudehard. Dark, acrid smoke of burning vehicles, and the stench of death and body parts created a horror scene reminiscent of Dante's Inferno. If there was a hell on earth, this was it!

The Germans now seeing they were terribly outnumbered, and their position like a cork in a bottle being hopeless, stopped fighting and surrendered by the thousands. Yet approximately 20,000 to 50,000 thousand fled under the cover of darkness leaving behind their heavy weapons, avoiding encirclement and almost certain destruction. They would later be reorganized and rearmed

in time to slow the Allied advance into Holland and
Germany.

This fierce battle in the Normandy campaign was
the beginning of the end of the war. The Canadians made a
wooden sign: 'A Polish Battlefield.' General Maczek
arrived in Chambois on 22 August to congratulate his
troops and witness the apocalyptic scene. A telegram was
read from General Crerar, Commander in Chief of the
Canadian Forces, 'First Canadian Army is proud to number
in its ranks 1st Polish Armoured Division.'

A private soldier stepped forward and offered
General Maczek an Iron Cross taken from a German
prisoner who had won it five years before against the
former Colonel Maczek, on the Polish battlefields. Maczek
on shaking hands with Colonel de Langlade, said: 'You are
a lucky man, Colonel. If you are killed in France, you will
die on your own liberated soil. We shall die on friendly
soil, but even so, foreign soil, and we shall never see
Poland again.'

Sgt. Edward Zyrmont, never saw Poland again.

Map of Europe in Daily Telegraph, 1941. Edek cut it out and wrote next to his home town in Poland 'Wolkowysk'-it was found in his breast pocket after his death. It was covered in black smoke.

Mont Ormel claimed the life of 330 Polish soldiers, 1000 wounded men, 87 tanks lost, but Polish persistence had won a great victory. Later, General Maczek said: 'God thus gave us the chance to take revenge on that unit which had fought in Poland in 1939, but this time the roles were reversed.'

This map was found in Edek's breast pocket when he was removed from his tank. It was a constant reminder of his beloved hometown. The paper was blackened by the smoke from the fire of his tank.

More than 40,000 inhabitants of Warsaw were killed by the Nazis; many were terrorized and tortured. The soldiers of the 1st Armoured Division, nicknamed the 'Black Devils,' by the Germans, had proudly earned their reputation for bravery. Montgomery had no choice but to praise them for their courage calling them, 'The cork in the bottle preventing the German escape.' Their revenge was very slow in coming, but extremely sweet. However, it would later prove to be sadly quixotic. The free Poland these soldiers dreamed of was only a distant dream!

Chapter Twenty-three

1944 - Maggie's Grief

Bella ran down the street to catch up with her sister who was on her way to Elsie's house. 'Maggie, this letter just arrived for you from the War Office.' She said in alarm.

Maggie turned white, and with a trembling hand tore it open. 'We regret to inform you of your husband Sgt. Edward Zyrmont's death. He was killed in action in France.' She took a deep breath and never let it out. A silent cry stuck in her throat like a hot liquid cutting off her oxygen.

Bella took her sister gently by the arm and led her in a catatonic state into their sister's house. Elsie took one look at Maggie's twisted face and crumpled paper in her hand, and instinctively knew. No words were needed. She ran into the kitchen to fetch a bottle of brandy.

'Here, dearie, sit down and drink this. I am so sorry.' Elsie said offering her a glass and a pillow for her back, then disappearing into the kitchen wiping her eyes. It broke her heart to see her sister in such despair.

Margaret slipped into the cushion of the armchair trying to digest what she had just read. Her body bent forward, the telegram still in her shaking hand as the words ripped through her soul like a searing hot iron. Her tears stained the paper as if to wash away the hurtful words:

'killed in action.' She dropped the letter in her lap not wishing to read another word, but her eyes kept returning to 'killed in action,' as if by staring at them her mind would finally accept that her beloved husband would never return to her. She was speechless, unable to absorb all the pain at once. Rationally, she knew he was dead, but emotionally he was very much alive in her heart. She had been so happy with him for such a short time. She knew instinctively when she kissed him goodbye at the station he had less of a passion for her and more of a zeal to fight to the death for Poland. It was in his blood. Now she would have to resign herself to her fate. She hated the brutality of war that had viciously robbed her of something she deeply loved.

Elsie brought her a cup of tea as Bella paced back and forth not knowing what to say to comfort her sister. 'Maybe I should go and tell Ma.' She whispered to Elsie.

'Oh, Elsie, he was so wonderful! He brought such happiness into my life. He was such a shining light. He taught me how to dance the tango, to speak Polish, to laugh, and left me with a beautiful little daughter. I am going to miss him so much. He had such charm and wit, but he didn't have time.' She said between sobs.

Alinka ran into the room, 'Why is Mommy crying?' She pulled on her mother's skirt. Only two, she could not understand the depth of sorrow. She was a happy baby surrounded by the love of a large family who spoiled her. And was too young to understand pain.

Auntie Elsie, unable to find the right words, muttered something about going into the kitchen to get a piece of chocolate cake. 'Bella, take the child into the kitchen and give her a glass of milk and some chocolate cake, then take her with you to granny's house. Maggie needs to be alone.'

Maggie was still in shock staring out the window watching the wind blow the leaves on the trees. Elsie rubbed her own tear-filled eyes, 'this war has brought so much heartache.'

Bella, put her arm around Maggie's shoulder trying to comfort her older sister who seemed so frail. 'We are all going to miss Edek. He was such a charmer, your dashing husband. I'll leave Alinka with granny for a few days so you won't have to look after her. I imagine you will not be going to work for a while. Do you want me to notify your boss?'

Maggie nodded her head. 'How do you tell a two-year old she will never see her daddy again?' She blew her nose in her handkerchief sobbing quietly.

'Best not to tell her. Why don't you stay with us tonight, dearie? I'll give you a pill to help you sleep. Come and I'll put you to bed in Kenneth's room and get a nice hot water bottle for your feet.' Elsie said putting her arm around her escorting her to her son's room, nodding to Bella to take the child away.

Elsie was terribly saddened by the unexpected events. Her poor sister, now a widow and barely twenty-four. When would this dreadful war end?

Maggie consoled herself reading Robbie Burns poetry: 'And fare thee weel, my only luve, And fare thee weel awhile! And I will come again, my luve, Though it were ten thousand mile.'

****

The days passed by painfully slow, then Maggie had to return to work while the two spinsters continued looking after the baby for her. On Sundays she would travel by bus with the baby to her mother's house where the Lindsays would congregate after church, but Jess did not dare play Chopin again for fear of reminding her sister of the happy times forever lost.

****

Maggie received a poignant letter from the men who had fought with her husband, it read:

On August 21, 1944, the Falaise Gap was closed when the Canadian 4th Armoured Division linked up with the 1st Polish Armoured Division.

By their sheer determination in holding their position, as ordered, against the German counterattack, the Poles were instrumental in closing the Falaise Gap, for which General Maczek was decorated.

After the Battle of the Falaise Gap, Montgomery was forced to admire and admit the bravery of this Division, which despite its heavy losses, was anxious to continue killing Germans.

On 06 September 1944, this Division crossed the Belgian frontier, with 'Vive la Polone,' as they were treated like heroes.

Despite further fighting and heavy losses, this Division fought all the way to Breda, The Netherlands, liberating their city on 29 October 1944.

Ferocious fighting continued for this distinguished Division, until the capitulation of the German Army on 5 May 1945.

The 1st Polish Armoured Division marched triumphantly to Wilhelmshaven. They had been brutally forced out of their beloved country, and many never returned.

As my stepdad had said, 'I fought against the Nazis, only to have my country stolen by the Communists. I have no country left!'

General Maczek also refused to return to a raped Poland. He lived in Scotland, and died on 11 December, 1994, at the age of 102. He is buried in Breda.

Edward Zyrmont, is buried in the Polish Military Cemetery at Grainville - Langannerie, France.

Polish Forces
E.L.A.
29th of December 1944.

Dear Mrs.Zyrmont,

    This is another letter for you which we write to tell you how p:
we are that your husband had fought with us.He had been one of the b.
viest a... ... ...er his gallant death.He gave his li..
our common cause fighting for " ..r and your freedom " .

    Believe us ... ...e share your good sorrow and regret tremendou:
his death as he belonged to our squadron's family which is for us a
dear one. We send you some money which have been collected by all of ₩
as a small token of our remembrance and we wish you in your life the
best of luck.-

                       Officers and other ranks
                       of his ... squadron.

3rd Squadron P/108
Polish Forces
B.L.A.
28th of December 1944

Dear Mrs. Zyrmont,

This is another letter for which we write to tell you how proud we are that your husband had fought with us. He had breviest and we shall always remember his gallant death. He gave his life in our common cause fighting for 'our and your freedom'.

Believe us that we share our great sorrow and regret tremendously his death as he belonged to our squadron's family which is for us a very dear one. We send you some money which we have been collected by all of us as a small token of our remembrance and we wish you in your life the very best of luck.

Officers and Other Ranks
Of the 3rd Squadron

General Stanislaw Maczek of the 1st Polish Armoured Division
being decorated for his victory of closing Falaise Gap

EPILOGUE

THE BRITISH RED CROSS SOCIETY

14 & 15 GROSVENOR CRESCENT
LONDON, S.W.I.

Telephone :
BELgravia 5454

Cables :
BRITREDCROSS. LONDON , S . W . l

Telegrams :
REDCROS, KNIGHTS, LONDON

Patron and President : HER MAJESTY THE QUEEN
Vice-President : HER MAJESTY QUEEN ELIZABETH THE QUEEN MOTHER

Executive Committee :
Chairman: THE RIGHT HON. THE EARL OF WOOLTON, P.C., C.H., D.L.
Vice-Chairman : THE COUNTESS OF LIMERICK, G.B.E.
Deputy Chairman : DAME ANNE BRYANS, D.B.E.
Secretary General : F. H. D. PRITCHARD, ESQ.

Our Ref:
Your Ref: MEW/RR/Polish

Date 11th December, 1961.

The Officer in Charge of Records,
The War Office Records Centre(Polish)
Bourne Avenue, Hayes, Middx.

Dear Sir,

We should be most grateful if you would be kind enough
to check your records for any mention of the following person:

1916/22/5 Edward ZYRMONT
son of Antoni and Antonina nee Pawluczuk
born 14.8.1916 ar 14.9.1916 at Mogilewcy/Bialystol

The enquiry is being made on behalf of:- his mother,
Mrs. Antonina Zyrmont in Poland.
We shall very much appreciate your help in this case and it
will be most useful to us if you are able to supply the Polish
Resettlement Corps number.

Yours faithfully

International Welfare Section
International Relations and Relief Department.

159

The Daily Telegraph

1 CANADA SQUARE   CANARY WHARF   LONDON E14 5DT
TELEPHONE 071-538 5000   TELEX: 22874 TELLDN G
DX42657 ISLE OF DOGS

November 22 1994

Dear Mrs Zyrmont. Lillian,

Thank you for your most moving letter, which I shall preserve.

I believe you might acquire some more information from the Sikorski Institute here in London, in Princes Gate, South Kensington S.W.7. You are probably already in touch with them.

There are hundreds of histories in Polish — do you read the language? I am sure the Sikorski Institute could give you titles.

I would be delighted to assist you further if I can. Please

Get in touch if the Sikorski
Institute cannot help as
needed.

I found your letter very
beautifully written.

Yours sincerely,

John Keegan

The Daily Telegraph
1 Canada Square Canary Wharf London E14 5Dt
November 22,1994
Dear Mrs. Zyrmont – Sullivan,

   Thank you for your most moving letter, which I shall preserve.

   I believe you might obtain some more information from the Sikorski Institute here in London in Princess Gate, South Kensington, S. W.7. You are probably already in touch with them.

   There are numerous histories in Polish – do you read the language? I am sure the Sikorski Institute would give you the titles.

I would be delighted to assist you further if I can. Please get in touch with me if the Sikorski Institute cannot help as needed.

I found your letter very beautifully written.

Yours Sincerely,
John Keegan

MONT ORMEL

"This is where the Polish Defended Our Freedom"

General S. Maczek, commanding the 1st Polish Armoured Division, which was part of the 1st Canadian Army, was ordered following Jort's push to strategic Chambois, an important road junction, and Montormel, Hill 262, at its highest point.

Capturing them would enable a linkup with the US Forces and the 2nd. French Armoured Division coming from the south, sealing off the Falaise-Chambois "pocket."

Roused by the Warsaw Uprising at the beginning of August, the Polish Forces reached Mont Ormel and the hill at Boisjos, after a lightening advance, on 19 August, 1944, around noon. They called the site "Maczuga" (the mass of weapons.) This armoured group comprised 2 tank regiments and 3 infantry battalions, in all,1800 men.

They were totally cut off. The intensity of the skirmishing with the enemy, the violence of the heavy artillery fire amid air bombings had prevented the 40th Canadian Armoured Division from reaching them. Colonel de Langlade's armoured group, 2nd. Armoured Division, and the 90th US Division were heavily engaged around Chambois.

The retreating Germans ran straight into the Polish Forces resulting in extremely fierce fighting. On several occasions, the Poles fighting hand-to-hand combated with bayonets.

On 20 August, they were caught in a cross-fire during a counter attack by the armoured units of the Das Reich's SS Armoured Division, retreating towards the outside of the "pocket" from Vimoutiers. However, despite suffering heavy casualties the Poles remained masters of the battlefield.

On the afternoon of 21 August, the first armoured units of the 4th Canadian Armoured Division succeeded in linking up with the besieged forces. The position became hopeless and the Germans gradually stopped fighting, surrendering in large numbers. Thousands fled under cover of darkness leaving their heavy weapons behind. This feat of arms brought the Normandy campaign to an end.

In addition to this, the permission granted to General Leclerc, to make for Paris, which was in the throes of an uprising with the 2nd. Armoured Division, allowed the capital to escape Warsaw's painful fate.

Edward Zyrmont's Decorations

A 'Black Devil' of the 1st Polish Armoured Division, Sgt. Edward Zyrmont, was the recipient of the following decorations:

1) Polish Krzyz Walecznych – (Cross for Valour) (Posthumously)
2) Polish Krzyz Zaslugi z Mteczami (Silver Cross with Swords) (P)
3) Medal Wojska (Army Service Medal) (P)
4) Polish Resistance in France Medal (P)
5) 1st Armoured Division Cross (P)
6) Ten Year Service Medal
7) Medal Commemorative Francaise De La Guerre 1939-45 Avec Barratte France (P)
8) France and Germany Star (P)
9) September 1939 Cross (P)
10) September 1939 Medal (P)
11) World War II Victory Medal (P)
12) World War II Veterans Freedom Cross and badge (P)
13) World War II Army Medal
14) Wounded Bar of Honour (P)
15) British 1939-45 Star (P)
16) British War Medal 1939-45 (P)
17) British Defence Medal 1939-45 (P)
18) Armoured Corps badge, pre-World War II
19) 2nd Armoured Battalion, pre-World War II
20) World War II 1st Armoured Regiment
21) World War II 2nd Armoured Regiment

22) World War II 10th Dragoon Armoured Regiment
23) 1st Armoured Division patch
24) 2nd Armoured Division badge
25) II Polish Corps badge
26) 2nd Warsaw Armoured Division badge
27) 8th British Army patch
28) World War II cap crowned eagle
29) World War II sword and belt, bayonet, rifle
30) World War II uniform with helmet, bayonet, rifle
31) World War II uniform with proper rank insignia
32) World War II Armoured Corps badge

'This is about 98% of his automatic entitlements.'

Prof. Z. Wesolowski

Bibliography

Archives

Polish Institute and General Sikorski Museum, 20 Princess
Gate, London, SW7 1PT, England, UK.

Correspondence

Sgt. Edward Zyrmont, photography and notes,
01 September 1939 to 20 August 1944.

3RD Squadron P/108, Polish Forces, B.L.A, 1944

Polski Czerwony Krzyz, Informacji I Poszukiwan,
Warszawa, Polonia, 1995.

The British Red Cross Society, 14 &15 Grosvenor
Crescent, London, S.W.1, England, UK, 1961.

Commonwealth War Graves Commission, 2 Marlow Road,
Maidenhead, Berkshire SL6 7DX, 1987.

Ministry of Defence, Bourne Avenue, Hayes, Middlesex
UB3 1RF, England, UK, 1995.

S. Grabowski, Kolo Kolezenskie 1-go Pulko Pancernego,
99 The Ridgway, London, W3 8LP, England, UK, 1994.

Polish-American Congress, Inc., 5711 N. Milwaukee
Avenue, Chicago, Ill. 60646, USA, 1995.

Wladyslaw Lis, 1st Polish Armoured Division, Veterans
Association, 5016 W. Cornelia Avenue, Chicago, Ill, USA,
postcode: 60641. 1995.

Borders Regional Council, Galashiels, Scotland, UK, 1995.

Numerous personal letters from the Zyrmont and Lazowski families in Gorzow, WLKP.

Various emails from Simon Roguszka, London, England, UK.

Embassy of the United States, Minsk, Belarus, 1995.

Secondary Sources

Blumenson, Martin, *The Battle of the Generals - The Untold Story of the Falaise Pocket – The Campaign That Should Have Won World War II: W. Morrow 1993.*

DeLauder, *The Falaise Pocket, World War II, Allied Encirclement of the German Armies, Failure or Success of the Allied Leadership and Planning:* Braden P. Publications, 2002.

Florentine, Eddy, *The Battle of the Falaise Gap: Elek Books 1965. (Originally published in 1964 under title: Stalingrad en Normandie.)*

Jamar K, *With the Tanks of the 1st Polish Armoured Division: H.L. SMIT & ZN.* – Hengelo, Holland, 1946.

Keegan, John, *Six Armies in Normandy: From D-Day to the Liberation of Paris, 06 June – 25 August 1944.* London, Jonathan Cape, 1982.

McGilvry, Evan, *The Black Devil's March – A Doomed Odyssey – The 1st Polish Armoured Division 1939-45:*

Helion and Company, Ltd., 26 Willow Road, Solihull, W. Midlands B91 1UE, England, UK. 2005.

Olof, Brian, *Easiguides – D-Day and the Liberation of Normandy: Self-drive Tour Guide, 1994.*

Journals and Newspapers

The Daily Telegraph, London, 1941 (map of Poland 1939). Telegraph Media Group Limited.

Weteran, November 1984, 17 Irving Place, N.Y., N.Y., 10003, USA.

World War II, *Imperfect Victory at Falaise,* Flint Whitlock, Leesburg, Virginia, USA.

The U.S. National Archives and Records Administration. Telephone: 1-866-272-6272.

External Links – Internet

The Killing Ground: The Battle of the Falaise Gap. Lucas, James Sidney, Barker, James: London, Batsford, 1978.

Fischer, Benjamin B, *The Katyn Controversy - Stalin's Killing Field. 4/13/2011:* www.cia.gov/library/center-for-the-study-of-intelligence-csi-publications/csi-studies.

Memorial de Coudehard – Montormel, France: http://www.memorial-montormel.org

FALAISE VICTORY

On French earth where red roses grow,

Their grey granite crosses stand in a row.

Dante's fiery hell cannot compare

To their own hell found untimely there,

With an enemy so despicably unfair.

He struck them down with his friends that day,

As the enemy cowardly ran fast away.

The heroes dreamed of freedom and liberty,

And of joyful Polish songs and gay festivity.

On blood-drenched fields in Falaise

They paid the price for a great victory.

Those granite crosses full of names

That now adorn their cold graves,

Of Poland's proud, youthful best,

With honour lie in an eternal rest.

Among them my dear unknown father,

Who lies with them in silent forever.

He knew me not, but heavenly powers

Are but years turned into lost hours.

For martyrs and heroes now are lain

In apple orchards where they were slain.

But in the house of a life with God,

Where only angels before had trod,

They sleep until a heavenly light

Awakes them all from the dark night,
Until their life infernal becomes life eternal.

Alicja Maria Zyrmont

ABOUT THE AUTHOR

Alicja Maria Zyrmont, has used the nom de plume Alinka Zyrmont for writing her novels, and travelogues on her website: www.alinkazyrmont.com

She was born in Dundee, Scotland, and educated in Buenos Aires, Argentina, later arriving in the United States where she attended Barry University and California College of Law. She presently lives in Arizona, USA, with her husband a retired commercial pilot.

In 1947, Margaret, the widow of Edward Zyrmont, married another Polish soldier in the Royal Air Force, Alexander Pawlowski, who became a Pan Am airline executive in Europe. He died in Warsaw and is buried in the Powazki Military Cemetery in Warsaw. He is survived by his son, Dr. Michael Alexander Pawlowski, from Texas.

It would be 54 years before Alinka found her family in Poland.

Printed in Great Britain
by Amazon

61720507R00116